PR F(

A Guidebook
To Publicity And Marketing

JEANNINE HALL GAILEY

Two Sylvias Press

Two Sylvias Press
PO Box 1524
Kingston, WA 98346
twosylviaspress@gmail.com

Cover Design: Kelli Russell Agodon
Book Design: Annette Spaulding-Convy
Author Photo: Tom Collicott

Created with the belief that *great writing is good for the world*, Two Sylvias Press mixes modern technology, classic style, and literary intellect with an eco-friendly heart. We draw our inspiration from the poetic literary talent of Sylvia Plath and the editorial business sense of Sylvia Beach. We are an independent press dedicated to publishing the exceptional voices of writers.

For more information about Two Sylvias Press please visit:
www.twosylviaspress.com

First Edition. Created in the United States of America.

ISBN: 978-1-948767-00-2

Two Sylvias Press
www.twosylviaspress.com

Acknowledgements

Thanks to my two lovely Two Sylvias editors, Kelli Russell Agodon and Annette Spaulding-Convy, for their tireless work and encouragement on this book's behalf. Without their push, it would never have been written!

Thanks to my husband Glenn Gailey and my mother Bettie Hall for reading early versions of the book, making suggestions, proofing, and encouragement. And thanks to Sylvia Andrea Nica for her hard work helping to copyedit this book.

Thanks to everyone who generously shared their resources in this book, including: Kelli Russell Agodon, Elizabeth Austen, Robert Lee Brewer, Sandra Beasley, Jeremy Brett, Victoria Chang, Serena Agusto-Cox, Heidi Czerwiec, Killian Czuba, Kelly Davio, Marie Gauthier, Anne Haines, Janet Holmes, Tom Hunley, Kelly Forsythe, Aimee Nezhukumatathil, Susan Rich, M.J. Rose, Chelsey Slattum, all my beta readers for their suggestions, and everyone who helped make this book a reality. I could not have done it without you.

Table Of Contents

PR FOR POETS

A Guidebook
To Publicity And Marketing

CHAPTER 1: WHAT IS PR FOR POETS?

Why Does A Poet Need To Know About PR?

You're a poet. And now you have become a *successful* poet. You have a poetry book contract in your hand, but you've been told one of the following false statements:

- Poetry doesn't sell.
- Poets shouldn't care about how well their work sells.
- Poets who do care about selling books are "sellouts," too concerned about "the Po-Biz," too "careerist," etc.

You didn't spend your time writing, revising, editing, and studying poetry *not* to have it in the hands of readers. Your goal in writing a book is to communicate your thoughts and ideas to people, to make an impact. In order for this happen, readers need to know that your book exists and is easily available for them to purchase.

You have worked hard: written, revised, and submitted your manuscript, then found a press who has given you a publication date. But part of being an author is doing what you can to get your book into the hands of readers. Your job isn't over yet; it has just begun. I want to help you break out of what's considered "the norm" and sell more than the usual 200-300 copies of your poetry book. While you may not have a press with a large marketing budget, if you are willing to do a fair amount of work, this guide will help you find your readers and ultimately, sell more books. Each of us has different resources—money, time, an existing fan base, or devoted friends and family—all of which can be used to launch our poetry books out into the world.

When I published my first book of poetry, *Becoming the Villainess*, I was thirty-two and in the middle of my MFA program. I already felt "over the hill" to be publishing a first book of poetry. Steel Toe Books, which published my first poetry collection, was a relatively new press and neither my publisher nor I were particularly sophisticated in the ways of PR or sales. But, we had some good luck, including a stint on the NPR show, *The Writer's Almanac,* as well as my book being taught in college level classes. This helped launch me into modest poetry success. With each book since then, I've learned a little bit more about what does and doesn't work in terms of selling a poetry book. Overall, I've felt happy with my sales numbers. I have poet friends who have sold over 10,000 copies of their poetry books—an ambitious number we should all aspire to in our journeys as poets.

What is *PR for Poets* about? What do I mean when I write about PR and marketing for poets? Don't be

2

frightened or offended by these terms; there's nothing about PR and marketing that's sleazy or terrifying—they are helpful tools for your success. This book will provide the information needed in order to get your book into the right hands and into the worlds of social media and old media, librarians and booksellers, and readers.

You do not need to wear a button that says "Ask me about my book!" or push your book onto unwilling strangers. I definitely don't want to turn you into a "shameless self-promoter," but instead, I want to help you become a smart professional author who is able to market your own book. One of the goals of *PR For Poets* is to consider the right (and wrong) ways to get the word out about your work.

One thing many new authors aren't aware of is that poetry books have a longer lifespan in terms of book reviews and word-of-mouth buzz than other genres, such as fiction or memoir. Because of this, marketing does not have to be frenetic nor unplanned. It also doesn't need to happen in a large, coordinated, expensive push over a two-month period. I will explore both the frustrations and hidden benefits of that longer lifespan.

There are some poets who sell a large number of books because of their influential and well-funded publishers, but these are a minority of the presses.

These presses have pull with bookstores and libraries because they are marketing books by a Pulitzer Prize winner or a former Poet Laureate of the United States. If you are Billy Collins, Mary Oliver, Rupi Kaur (the "Instagram poet"), or Ocean Vuong, you probably don't need this book. But, even if you have signed with a dream press, you may still need to know the basics of navigating the world as a poetry author.

One of the reasons I decided to write *PR for Poets* is because there are so few resources out there for writers like ourselves—hardly anyone mentions poetry when they talk book promotion or marketing. Poetry is a specialized, niche market with its own boosters, reviewers, and publications. There was no one to tell me if buying an ad in *Poets & Writers* (as opposed to other, smaller publications) was worth the money, or who in major media might be interested in poetry books. I checked out many publications from the library on PR and book promotion and was disappointed to see how little of the advice applied to poets and our genre. This book will offer you help in setting expectations and avoiding pitfalls, providing you with tips for social media and readings. Lastly, I hope *PR For Poets* will empower you to do what you can to connect your poetry book with its audience!

CHAPTER 2: SHEDDING THE SHAME OF PR

Why You Shouldn't Worry About Promoting Your Book

It's easy to understand why you may not be excited about promoting your work. In my experience, most poets are introverts, and therefore not excited about the "self-promotion" part of publishing a book. In addition, some poets are surprised when their publishers (especially small presses) expect them to pitch in on behalf of their own book. Many times we writers enjoy the process of writing, but we don't necessarily like all of the other activities (giving readings, talking about our books, using social media, etc.) that are needed to connect readers with our books. Personally, I'd much rather be typing away on my laptop than setting up a reading or making small talk at a party. On the other hand, you should realize that the more work you do to get your writing into people's hands (and minds, and hearts), the greater the impact your art can have on the lives of others.

I frequently joke with other writers "we're not pushing harmful drugs on people—we're pushing a beautiful art form that might actually enhance lives." The hours you've invested in each book you've written, each poem you've crafted, will pay off as more and more people discuss and talk about your work. In order for this to happen, you will need to do readings, visit book clubs, guest-teach workshops, get on social media. But it will be worth it!

Just say to yourself "WWWWD." (What would Walt Whitman do?) Whitman famously wrote and published a glowing review of his own seminal collection *Leaves of Grass* when the work was not receiving the acclaim he felt it deserved. This is obviously not something that I'm going to recommend in this book, but it gives you an idea of how desperate even canonized writers can be to promote their work.

The following is a quote from author and editor Kelli Russell Agodon, who has given me this kind of pep talk many times:

When little kids run up to show us a picture they have drawn or want to read their short story to anyone who will listen, we do not think, "shameless self-promoter"—but we are instead charmed by their excitement and their creation. Somehow as adults, we've forgotten this second part of creating something—sharing it. Our minds may get in the way of our poet-hearts and instead of sharing our work, we hide it or downplay it.

As writers and artists, we need to be the excited child with our work and share our work in a way that is devoid of ego, but in the absolute pleasure of being a human who has created something new. We need to mention what we've finished, what we've done, without our internal critic telling us "You don't deserve this," or asking, "Who do you think you are?"

You are an artist. You are a writer. You are someone who has dedicated a large amount of your time to not only writing a poem, but to putting together an entire book of these poems. You not only wrote it, but you finished it! And now, you deserve to share it (and with joy).

Yes, it's hard to put the spotlight on yourself, but I'm not suggesting a spotlight. I'm suggesting holding a candle up to your work and letting the glow surround it. I'm suggesting that you take your book out into the sunlight or under the light of the moon. See what happens. See who notices.

Believe that it's okay to share your work. Let others know you have a new book in the world without hesitation and without worrying about your sales numbers. It's not about selling books or being the best; it's about making art and letting your book find its readers. The gift of art is in the creating and the connecting, so share with the childlike delight of having created something new. Send your books and poems out knowing you have added a little more art to the world and find the beauty, satisfaction and fulfillment in the art, not in the end result.

CHAPTER 3: SETTING EXPECTATIONS

What's A Reasonable Result For My PR Efforts?

Before we dive into the basics of book promotion, I want to take one brief chapter to help you understand the reasonable expectations for a poet to have regarding a new book. I don't want this to be a downer or take the wind out of your sails. The process is just better when you know what to expect.

On Facebook in 2015, *Rattle* editor and poet Tim Green posted the following:

In five years, Red Hen Press has sold 105 copies of my book. This doesn't include my own copies that I've sold or given away, maybe 200, but still—105 copies, despite the fact that it's a fairly good book, and that I have a fairly large "platform" within the poetry community. More people will read this Facebook post in the next 20 minutes than will have read that book. This is why I don't get all that jazzed about publishing anymore.

To put it another way: When I think about having published a book, my primary emotion is guilt—guilt that I didn't do more for the book, for the sake of the press. You have to work as an author, and I don't care enough about publishing my poems to work it like that.

I believe that there are many poets out there who feel exactly like this. We wonder what, exactly, are reasonable sales expectations for a poetry book. What kind of promotion can your publisher reasonably expect you to do? What is the publisher going to be able to do for you? What is out of the author's hands totally? As we discuss these questions, I hope you can benefit from my experience.

Based on the poetry publishers I've spoken with over the years, Tim's number, around 300 total sales over five years, is fairly normal for poetry book sales. It's rare for a poetry book to break 1,000 copies, rarer still to get to 10,000. Only people who win the gigantic prizes and former Poet Laureates make it higher than that. Your famous poets (think Mary Oliver, Billy Collins, Louise Gluck) sell poetry books in numbers that make a profit for non print-on-demand printing runs. The rest of us? Well, it's more normal to struggle than not to struggle.

As I was gearing up to promote my fourth book, I wondered about what I've learned and how I could apply it. What is the best use of my time, energy, and money in terms of promoting my book? Every book has had different successes. My bestselling book is still my first book, *Becoming the Villainess*, which has been taught in college classes. However, my fifth book, *Field Guide to the End of the World*, is catching up, probably due to better distribution. All five of my publishers have been small, independent presses without a PR department or much funding for ads, tours, etc. It's likely that many of you are in the same position, and maybe that's why you've purchased this book.

When it comes to promoting your poetry book, consider what you're willing to do, what you can afford to do, and how much energy you have for promotion. Also consider how long you plan to promote your book. 2013, for instance, was the first year for *Unexplained Fevers*, and the seventh year for *Becoming the Villainess*, and *Becoming the Villainess* still outsold *Unexplained Fevers*, even though I was actively promoting the new book. There's a momentum to poetry book sales, which, once it takes off, starts to have a life of its own. That's what you want, and what you will get when you are both persistent and just a little lucky.

If you teach or if you're an editor for a literary magazine or small press, you may have a better "platform" from which to sell books. But it's not automatic; you still have to send out your email announcements to your email lists, send out your postcards, go sell books at conferences, set up your readings where you're fairly sure you will have an audience, like your hometown or your MFA program. You don't control the critical reception for your book, although you can help send out review copies to interested reviewers, or you can provide your publisher a list of likely review places. You may not be able to afford a cross-country reading tour, but the good news is, those things may not be necessary. Social media and online ads are beginning to replace some of the old-fashioned promotion techniques.

And what can create the kind of angst Tim talks about, is that no one ever tells you, "This is enough. You've done enough." Even poets with successful books (or that I consider pretty darn successful) feel that pressure. When do you give yourself a break?

Once, publishers had PR people, funded tours, and bought ads in big magazines. Now, very few publishers can afford to do that, and they only do it for a few of their books. So, a lot more responsibility comes back on us, the writers, than it used to.

Janet Holmes, director and editor of Ashanta Press, states that sales of their books tend to range from 700 -1000 copies, with some of the more successful authors selling more. Janet shared with me the welcome kit that Ashanta provides to each of its authors to help them generate sales for the press. I was gratified to see in their welcome kit many of the same PR suggestions and insights that I have already included in this book. Ashanta also sends out more than 150 review copies of their titles, which is an exceptional number.

There are times when you will be able to invest extra time and cash in your book and times when you won't be able to. Life can get in the way, preventing you from really promoting your book. It's my hope that *PR for Poets* will help you do so as efficiently as possible, no matter your current situation.

CHAPTER 4: PARTNER WITH YOUR PUBLISHER

Is My Publisher The Right One For My Book?

I decided to include this section because most of us as are so excited when we finally get our book accepted for publication that we don't ask key questions about promotion and distribution. Remember that most small publishers typically have neither the manpower nor the budget to do much, but they should be willing to do what they can!

I get lots of mail from poets asking about how to get a book published. But here is a question poets often don't ask themselves, "What am *I* looking for in a poetry publisher?" I think this is something we should give more thought to before we begin sending out our manuscripts. When a poet's first book is accepted, there is so much excitement that the poet often expects more from a publisher than the publisher's resources allow. Some people express frustration at a system that requires writers to pay for the privilege of having an editor or publisher even glance at their work. Of my five books, only one was published through a book contest. The other four were selected through an open submission process. I like supporting small publishers, but there are pluses and minuses to every decision we make about our books. However, we actually have a lot more control than we think.

Putting together your first book of poetry, you may look at a list of first-book contests, which are the most numerous and often the most prestigious, and wonder: "Should I part with the $25 contest fee for a ticket to an expensive, low-paying lottery? Or should I do research by attending literary fairs or conferences, finding micro or small publishers who might be friendly to my aesthetic? Should I wait until a major bookfair and take a look at some of the books on sale, trying to find a publisher that offers the kind of design and content I like?"

After your first book, there are fewer contest options. I have included a list of resources at the end of this book, including Tom Holmes and Rachel Dacus's online suggestions for publishers. I particularly like both of their lists.

You will want to take a look at the books a press produces BEFORE signing up to publish with them. If you are able, try to attend a major poetry festival like Portland's Wordstock, the Dodge Festival in New Jersey, or the Skagit River Poetry Festival in Washington. Consider attending a major bookfair like those held in L.A. or Miami, or the annual conference of the Association of Writers & Writing Programs (AWP), one of the largest annual gatherings of poetry and small press publishers. At these events, you can often meet the editors themselves, or at least get a better feel for what they are looking for. If you can't attend a festival or bookfair, maybe you can take advantage of the selection at a poetry-only bookstore like Seattle's Open Books, Harvard's Grolier Poetry Bookshop, Boulder's Innisfree Poetry Bookstore, or a local poetry-friendly independent bookstore. Otherwise, you can always order books directly from the publishers that you are targeting.

What are the most important things you hope your publisher can do for your book? Is their distribution good enough? What about a dedicated marketing department or PR service? Or is your priority that you want to work closely with a friendly editor who loves and is enthusiastic about your work? Do you want to help promote a new publisher and do extra work to get the word out about both their press and your new book? Do you care about the royalty statement, prize money, or profits? Have their books won prestigious prizes? Do you even care about prestige? Can they afford to buy ads or do any promotion? What about review copies? Do you get input on your book's cover art? Do they have a decent website and use social media? Are their books available on Amazon? Or do you want to do everything yourself and self-publish? Some of these questions may be more important to you than others, so it's important to know your priorities as you look for a publisher for your manuscript.

I have a friend who will remain nameless, who sent out his book manuscript for a long time. Lots of years. I had the opportunity to read it, and I knew it was excellent. I was anxious for him to get it out into the world, so I advised him to look for a smaller publisher and not to concentrate only on the big poetry book contests. Still, he persevered. He won the Yale Younger Poet's Prize. So, ha ha, joke's on me. Don't take my advice if you're about to win the Yale Younger Poet's Prize.

It's something to think about—sometimes we are in such a rush for publication that we may miss out on some larger opportunities that would have come if we had more patience or took more time crafting our books. Know what's important to you: Do you want to persevere believing that your manuscript will be chosen by a prestigious prize? Would you be okay with a lesser-known prize or press if it means getting your work out in the world earlier? As authors, we each have different ideas for what is best for us—know yourself well enough to choose the best path for yourself.

Here are some of the important items to research regarding your publisher:

- **Distribution**: Distribution is key for getting

books sold online and in bookstores without having to sell them yourself. Find out who your publisher's distributor is, and make sure your book will be available on Amazon.

- **Royalties**: Royalties vary a lot between publishers—some publishers don't pay any while others pay in copies. Many times, if you receive prize money for winning a book prize, the payment is in lieu of royalties. This prize money might be more than a poet would receive from a lifetime of royalties and it keeps accounting at a minimum for a small press. Sometimes a press will offer prize money and a royalty contract, other times, you will receive royalties after you've sold a certain number of books. Read your contract closely—the details about your payment are stated there.

- **Author and Review Copies**: Sending printed books to key reviewers and media outlets is a good way to put your book in the hands of people who can promote you. Ask your press if they will send out review copies (or a certain number of review copies). Remember that most presses are happy to email digital PDFs as review copies. Also, most presses will allow you to buy copies of your book at an author discount. Again, this is usually stated in your contract, but if you have any questions, ask your press for this information.

- **Promotion**: While a large publisher may be willing to sponsor a book launch party, cover some of your travel expenses for readings, or spring for promotional items such as postcards, bookmarks, and other "swag," many presses do not have large budgets for promotion of poetry books. Communicate with your press to explore what they are able to do and how you can help as well. I've shared the cost of print ads with several of my publishers. This may be a good solution for smaller presses who want to do more for your book, but may not have the resources.

- **Contests**: Once your book is published, winning a book prize, such as a state book award, a Foreword Indie Book Prize, or even a National Book Prize, can be great for promotion, but entry fees can be expensive and sometimes a gamble. Determine how much you (and your publisher) are willing to spend on book prizes and which book prizes are the best fit for your book. Some publishers may be able to help out with the fees or at least provide the required book copies.

- **Book Design**: The design, and especially the cover art, of a book matters to many writers, including me. If it matters to you, find out if you get a say in the design and cover art of your book. Many publishers choose your cover art and design your book without your input, while others view the book cover as a collaboration. Either way, remember that book designers are skilled at creating innovative covers, so listen to their edits and suggestions so that your book will look professional and eye-catching.

- **Timelines**: Timelines can vary between presses. One press may have your chapbook published in eight months, while another press could take a year and half. Most presses take anywhere from one to two years from the time you submit the final version of your manuscript until publication. And sometimes with small presses, things may end up going more slowly than expected. Ask your press if they have a release date they are aiming for, since this affects the PR calendar for your book.

Publishers want the best for your book. Though some have limited resources when it comes to promotion and marketing, they will be enthusiastic about your book and most are connected to a robust network of bookstores and reviewers. Smaller presses may be open to working with the author as far as splitting larger print ad costs or entry fees for published book contests. Communicate with your press and be open with your goals for your book. Also realize that even larger publishers are limited in their resources these days, so anything you do to help promote your book will be appreciated. And if you sell more books through your efforts, your press will be more likely to publish your next book, which will save you time and money in looking for a new publisher.

CHAPTER 5: PREPARING FOR SUCCESS

What You Can Do Before Your Book Is Published

Not everyone who reads this book will have a full-length book contract in hand. Maybe you have just released your chapbook, and you've started thinking about producing a full-length manuscript. Maybe you've got a full-length manuscript that you've been sending out, and you've got a handful of "finalist" listings, and you're ready to start prepping for your eventual debut. If you don't have your book yet, that doesn't mean that you can't start preparing to market your future work. In fact, I recommend it, especially if you are serious about getting your book out there. It's better to be over-prepared. Here are some book promotion basics you can start with, even before you've received your book contract. I'll expand on these PR basics in subsequent chapters.

Build Community

While you will sell books to readers who aren't personally acquainted with you, your community is a great starting point when looking for readers who are interested in your work.

Building a community has benefits even if your focus isn't about PR and promoting a book. Whether your community consists of your MFA companions, your hometown friends, your high school and/or college classmates, your writing group—be sure that you are meeting new people and doing what you can to have a stable and positive troupe of individuals who want to help you. And a lot of that comes from *you helping them*. It should be a mutually beneficial relationship. These are the people who will want to support you by buying your book.

Making friends in the writing world can seem intimidating. The community of writers might appear like a cold, combative, competitive place. But it does not have to be. Consider these strategies, both online and in-person, for reaching out to other writers and building your community of peers:

- Write reviews of other poets' books and submit them to print journals, online journals, or post them on your own blog or on Amazon.

- Attend poetry events in your local area. Other writers will appreciate your support.

- Volunteer at a local literary magazine or literary center. You'll be amazed at the supportive friends you'll make "in the trenches."

- Offer to start a local writers' group if you're not already in one. You will not only help each other perfect your poems, but you will encourage each other to submit work. There will also be mutual comfort in rejection and mutual praise for success.

- Attend regional or national poetry festivals or writing conferences. This can be expensive, but it's a great way to personally connect with your peers whom you would not otherwise get to meet.

I promise you that the karma from doing good in the poetry world will often come back to you.

Build A Platform

In book marketing, your platform is something you build before you need it, so you can take the leap when it's time to promote your book. I'm going to say this now: Create a professional author website and set it up *before* you get your book deal. It will help your Google "searchability" and it will help people, like reviewers and editors, contact you.

There's plenty to do when building a platform— creating your website, choosing your author email, and building mailing lists. We'll go over each of these in detail in later chapters.

Build A Social Media Presence

How important is social media for poets? Well, it can consume all your writing time, but it can also be very helpful in making poetry friends across the globe, in getting reviews, and selling books. There are now dozens of social media outlets. Here is a list of the most popular platforms:

- Facebook
- Blogger
- Twitter
- LinkedIn
- Tumblr
- Instagram
- Pinterest

You should find the combination of social media outlets that best match your community and lifestyle, since they are the places you will reach people—friends, family, and fans. The key is to figure out what works for you and to be consistent in a couple of these social media outlets (you'll go crazy trying to handle them all). I'll cover this in detail in *Chapter 12: Social Media and Blogs*.

Action Items:

1. Make a list of what you can start doing to build your presence online and in the community. Do you have a website? Compile a list of mailing addresses and email addresses of people who might be interested in your book. Are you currently part of a writing group?

2. Write down five questions that you will ask a publisher when you receive a book offer or questions that you would like to ask your current publisher now.

3. Make a list of the areas that need improvement in preparation for your book being released: Are you active on social media? Have you thought about scheduling in-person events? Have you started an email list? Are you currently giving readings?

4. Make a list of the areas where you feel confident in terms of promoting your book.

CHAPTER 6: READY TO LAUNCH

What To Do After You Sign Your Book Deal

You have your book deal. You win a contest. A publisher contacts you from their open submission season and informs you that they want to publish your book. You need to get marketing materials for your book together so that you can hit the ground running. In this chapter, we'll discuss mailing lists, author photos, and PR and pitch kits.

Get A Professional Author Photo

Nope, I'm not kidding. You'd be surprised how often you'll need a high-quality author photo (or "headshot") as you put together your PR and review kit, your website, and your social media accounts. Your author photo will most likely appear on the back of your book. You should have a high-quality headshot ready to go as soon as possible.

If you happen to have a professional photographer as a friend, this is a chance to hire him/her or offer to trade services. If you do not have professional photographer friends, consider hiring someone who does headshots for local business people or find the photographer who has taken a local author's photo which you think is high-quality. Selfies are okay for Facebook, but they have their limits, and they probably aren't what you want for a professional image. If you are on a budget, ask a friend or partner with a good digital camera (and good lighting) to take some shots of you.

I've seen a lot of interesting author photos. These are just my suggestions, but in your headshot, you might want to avoid the following:

- Cats
- Dogs
- Lingerie (you would think this is an obvious one)
- Weird hats (unless you always wear a weird hat)
- Cheesy pull-down photo studio backdrops
- A background of bookcases (not because it looks bad, but because everyone does it)

Here are some better options:

- Use natural lighting, which can be surprisingly flattering.
- Find poses and backgrounds that are classic, not trendy.
- Choose clothing you would actually wear to a reading.
- Consider professional help with your hair and makeup. The goal here is to be able to make you feel confident, to let people get an idea of the "real you," whatever that looks like.

- Google or look at author photos on the back of poetry books you admire, and consider what is making their shot work. Try using those techniques in your own photo.

The idea for your headshot is not to get a "glamour shot," but to show how you would look on the day of a reading or a media event; you, with the volume turned up just a little. Most of us aren't crazy about getting our pictures taken (hey, there's a reason we're writers, not supermodels), but we need these photos for the backs of books, websites, press kits, and social media accounts. People want to be able to connect to an author they admire. I try to update my author photo every couple of years, because I don't want to be one of those authors with a fifteen-year-old author photo, where you think, "Who is this person?" when you meet them.

Think About Blurbs

Blurbs are the short quotes written about your book by other writers, which appear on the back cover or on the inside jacket. Blurbs are a great way to advertise what readers will find in your book. Seeing positive comments from a well-known writer can also reassure potential buyers about the quality of the work. The more well-known the writer, the more effective the blurb. A large and influential publisher may be able to get a few of its top-shelf authors to write blurbs for you, but with small publishers, getting the blurbs is often left up to the poet. If your publisher can't help, contact the most esteemed of your poet friends and colleagues and ask if they would be willing to write blurbs for you (and don't be hurt or discouraged if some say "no"). I've known poets who directly asked well-known writers (whom they didn't know) for blurbs with a successful result, but this doesn't always happen. If you are wrangling your own blurbs, find out from your publisher when they are due, and give the poets writing your blurbs plenty of time to respond. Remember, they are doing you a favor, and your blurbs may not be at the top of their "to do" list.

Assemble Your Mailing Lists

Get your mailing lists—both email and snail mail—in order. This includes everyone on your holiday card list, all your extended family members, old friends, writing buddies, and the nice people who might have written to you to mention how much they like your work. Every time someone hands you their business card, it goes on the mailing list. Every person who orders a copy of your book gets added to your mailing list. When your publisher asks you for your mailing list so that they can send out postcards or other marketing materials, you want to have this list ready.

How do you go about building a mailing list? Put out a clipboard at your public events, and let people know they can sign up for news about your new book. When someone writes you to tell you how much they enjoyed a poem of yours or a reading, ask if you can include them on your mailing list. Some people build forms for their websites that people can use to sign up for a mailing list. You can also assume everyone you invite over to parties at your house (your second cousin, your hairdresser, your best friend from grad school) will want to be on your mailing list.

You want email information *and* mailing address information, because you'll be letting these people know about your book in two mediums—print and online. You may also want to start an account with TinyLetter, a free newsletter service so fans and readers can sign up to learn more about your work. Make the link for the newsletter available on your website so visitors can subscribe.

Create A Reviewer List

While a mailing list can be very broad (anyone who might be interested in your book) there is another important list: places and people who may want to review your book. This list might include your local newspaper, your alumni newsletter, literary magazines that have published work appearing in your book, and reviewers who have reviewed books similar to your work in style or subject. Include the media outlets you might not have a close relationship with, but who may be interested in reviewing or talking about your book. People on this list can be sent a review kit, which we'll discuss in *Chapter 7: PR Kits and Pitch Letters.*

Get The Word Out!

You built your community? Right! Now, it's time to let your community know your book is out. If you have good writer friends, ask them to help you get the word out through their social networks. Invite them over to a pre-book launch party or post-book launch party. Get their advice on how to get your book into a certain bookstore and brainstorm possible reading venues. In the following chapters, I will discuss more specifics about getting the word out for your new book.

Action Items:

1. Talk to writer friends or family and find out if anyone knows a professional photographer whom they would recommend for your author photo. If this isn't an option, arrange for a friend or partner to take your photo with a good digital camera.

2. Think about who you would love to have blurb or review your book. It helps to plan in advance. Do you read poetry book reviews? If not, now is a great time to start looking at the poetry reviews in publications such as *Rain Taxi, The Rumpus*, and *The Women's Review of Books*, for a start.

3. Hanging out in bookstores and at other poets' readings and book launch parties are great ways to invest in your poetry community. Start now!

CHAPTER 7: PR KITS AND PITCH LETTERS

Do It Yourself or Hire Someone?

In this chapter, I'll answer the questions: "What is a PR Kit? What is a pitch letter? Do I have to do these myself? What's my publisher's role? Can I hire someone to do it?"

If you haven't worked as a journalist, reviewer, or in publishing before, you may not be familiar with a PR kit. A PR kit, also known as a media kit, is a collection of physical or digital marketing materials designed to get the attention of the media. PR kits are sent to traditional media outlets, such as newspapers, radio and TV stations, journalists, and prominent bloggers. A pitch letter usually accompanies the kit and is the hook that piques the recipient's interest. Pitch letters are critical when you don't have a relationship with the person or organization receiving your kit. Your kit can be in a digital format (often a PDF file), which is usually sent by email or made available for download from a website. Some outlets still require that a hardcopy be mailed.

Your Basic PR Kit And "Sell Sheet"

The basic PR kit includes a "sell sheet," which is usually a single sheet, sometimes printed on both sides (often in color). Your sell sheet can be both digital and in hardcopy. It should include the following information:

- **Key data for your book**—this includes the publisher, distributor, release date, number of pages, format, ISBN number, website, and the PR contact. This provides important information about the book and facilitates the ordering process for libraries, bookstores, and universities/schools.

- **A summary of the book**—this is usually 200 words describing the breadth of the work. It's important to be broadly descriptive because many of the blurbs will hone in on specific aspects.

- **A graphic of the book's cover**—because color images have more impact, you may want to spend extra on color copies or borrow the color laser printer at work for your hardcopy version.

- **One or two blurbs**—these blurbs are short and only consist of a sentence or two. They present different facets of the work not covered in the summary. Pick the most famous of your blurbers to feature. Sometimes this choice is up to your publisher, not you.

- **Your author photo**—hopefully you already have this, so it's time to use it.

- **A short author bio**—really, keep this short. Include only your key accomplishments or items that might hook the specific reader (for example, if you are from his/her home town).

Where To Send The Sell Sheet

This sell sheet, printed in color, should be sent to bookstores, your former schools, your local community, and any other places that would want details about your book. I also include this sheet with every review copy of my book that is sent out.

Extending the PR Kit

There are several other kinds of marketing materials that you may want to add to your PR kit, including the two following items:

- **An Author Questionnaire**—this is usually a single page of questions and answers that relate to your book or you as an author. The purpose of the questionnaire is to make it easier for journalists and interviewers to write about your work and to prepare to interview you. It's often a good idea to target this Q & A for specific media markets, such as hometown papers (include questions that focus on your local connections) or topics included in your book, for instance, environmental journals (include questions that focus on the environmental facets of your work).

- **An E-Galley**—this is an electronic version of your book often created in portable document format (PDF), which is sent out to reviewers. The e-galley is usually ready when the book is in the process of being sent to the printer, so ask your publisher for a copy.

"PR Kit" Plus "E-Galley" Equals "Review Kit"

The PR kit along with your book's e-galley is sometimes called a "review kit." You can send out a digital version of this to your friends who have blogs, people whose book reviews you admire, and the publications that have published your work before. If you're not sure if you should send your "review kit," ask first! If people aren't interested, fine. Sending our your review kit as early as possible—three to six months in advance of your book coming out—is ideal. Many reviewers will also request a print copy of your book, so you may want to talk with your publisher to clarify who will handle sending out print review copies of your book. Some special kinds of contests, such as those run by writing associations, require you to make an e-galley available to members for voting on your book. But, in general, it's not a good idea to widely distribute an e-galley, since it can be used to produce a black market copy of your book. We'll talk more about how to get your book reviewed in *Chapter 15: Pursue the Elusive Review*.

—FOR IMMEDIATE RELEASE—

THE ROBOT SCIENTIST'S DAUGHTER

Poems by Jeannine Hall Gailey

"WE ARE WITNESSING A BRILLIANT
PERFORMANCE."
—Ilya Kaminsky, *Dancing in Odessa*

"FULL OF FLOWERS AND COMPUTERS, THIS RIV-
ETING POETRY CAPTURES THE UNDENIABLE COM-
PROMISES AND COMPLEXITIES OF OUR TIMES."
—Denise Duhamel, *Blowout*

Dazzling in its descriptions of a natural world imperiled by our nuclear past, *The Robot Scientist's Daughter* presents a girl in search of the secrets of survival. Within its pages, poet and writer Jeannine Hall Gailey describes a world of radioactive wasps, cesium infused sunflowers, and robotic daughters, conjuring an intricate menace of the nuclear family and nuclear history.

Mining her experiences as a child growing up in Oak Ridge, Tennessee—"The Atomic City"—Gailey weaves together stories of the creation of the first atomic bomb, the unintended consequences of scientific discovery, and time spent building nests for birds in the crooks of maple trees to create a reality at once terrifying and beautiful. *The Robot Scientist's Daughter* reveals the underside of the Manhattan Project from a personal angle, and charts a woman's—and America's—journey towards reinvention.

Jeannine Hall Gailey served as the second Poet Laureate of Redmond, Washington. She is the author of three additional books of poetry: *Becoming the Villainess*, *She Returns to the Floating World*, and *Unexplained Fevers*. Her poems have appeared in *The American Poetry Review*, *Prairie Schooner*, and *The Year's Best Horror*, and have been featured on NPR's "The Writer's Almanac". For more information visit www.webbish6.com.

MARCH 1, 2015
—MAYAPPLE PRESS—
6 x 9 | pp 82
Trade Paper | US $15.95
ISBN-13: 978-1936419425

Distributed by
Small Press Distribution

FOR ALL MEDIA QUERIES CONTACT:
Jeannine Gailey
jeannine.gailey@gmail.com

 MAYAPPLE PRESS | 362 CHESTNUT HILL RD, WOODSTOCK, NY 12498 | (845) 684 5599 | WWW.MAYAPPLEPRESS.COM

PAGE 1 OF 3

Figure 1: Page one of an extended PR kit

Pitch Letters

A pitch letter is written to get the attention of someone in book media. The pitch letter is similar to the cover letter you use when submitting your resume; it's intended to entice the recipient into taking a hard look at your PR kit. In your pitch, consider providing the recipients with a story angle or a hook that may link your book to relevant stories they are working on. For example: "Dear media representative (use a name, if possible), It's the anniversary of Hurricane Katrina, and my book, *Hurricane Katrina*, is an inside look at the events…" Keep your pitch letter short and sweet and to the point, and make sure you have links to all relevant information. On the following page is an example of one of my pitch letters:

Dear media contact,

I'm writing to see if you might be interested in a review of a short collection of poetry called *The Robot Scientist's Daughter* from a female-run press (Mayapple Press) that's coming out in March 2015. The collection follows a girl growing up in "America's Secret City" of Oak Ridge, Tennessee, and the fallout of nuclear families and our country's nuclear history. My father worked for Oak Ridge National Laboratories as a robotics expert on nuclear waste cleanup when I was a child, and I studied biology to learn more about the damage that nuclear experimentation can do to people and the environment. I also wanted to capture the pop cultural representations of atomic history, robots, and mad scientists (and their daughters.) I hope it will connect with your readers.

I'll be on a national tour for this book, my fourth collection of poetry, in the spring of 2015. I recently served as Poet Laureate of Redmond, Washington and have published three previous poetry books on women characters in folk tales, comic books, and video games. My website is www.webbish6.com and I'm on Twitter @webbish6.

Thank you so much for your time and consideration!
Jeannine Hall Gailey

Hard-copy ARCs and e-galleys are available upon request. My press kit is available from Mayapple Press or from this link from my website: http://www.webbish6.com/rsd/presskit

Figure 2: Example pitch letter

Doesn't My Publisher Do This?

At this point, you might be saying to yourself, "I'm not a PR professional. Isn't my publisher supposed to do this?" Sometimes your publisher will be able to do this for you. They may have resources and experience in writing pitch letters. If so, terrific! But sometimes, (or much of the time) your publisher won't have the resources to do this for you. It might be up to you to create the pitch letter and send it to media professionals, reviewers, and others so that they can learn about your book.

Can't I Just Hire Someone To Do This?

"Should I try to create these materials myself or hire someone to do it for me so it looks professional?" This is another great question! When you feel like you don't have time, energy, or desire to do this kind of PR for your book, you may wonder if you can hire someone to take care of everything for you. The answer is: "Sort of, and it depends." You'll probably still have to help the publisher put together a Q&A for the publicity materials, do readings, ask contacts for blurbs, etc. And, even if you have a dedicated PR person, they will need your input to do their job effectively.

A PR person who does all your work—from arranging readings, reviews, and media contact pitches—can cost quite a bit of money, probably much more than most poets will receive from sales and royalties. A good reputable book PR person might charge between five to twenty thousand dollars to help promote your book. Ouch, right? That's one of the reasons I decided to write this book! There are also "cut rate," less expensive PR services that offer to help you promote your book—I see these services advertised on Twitter quite a bit—but they likely won't be able to target a poet's specific audiences. Sometimes you get what you pay for.

I was one of those poets who thought: *Isn't there someone who can help me*? I read a ton of materials on book publicity, interviewed many people who work in PR, and talked to many publishers and authors about strategies that worked for them. Even with my wealth of experience, I'm still learning! Methods and platforms are changing all the time, and the things that worked like a charm ten years ago don't always work today with contemporary audiences. Also, recessions or trends can affect you even if you have done the right work the right way.

I have met reputable PR people who do work with poets. Recently one set up a reading that involved a poet from the East Coast who was on her book tour and me. Both the poet and the PR person were gracious and good potential contacts for the future. Sometimes, poets who have more money than time pay a PR person to do their book mailings, set up readings, or send their book info out to media sources. It is harder to find a PR person who will work with poets, and rarer for a PR person to be familiar with the world of poetry (for the simple reason that poetry is a small part of the market that doesn't usually bring in much money). But if you find a PR person, and you have extra cash but not excess time, feel free to give him/her a try—and let me know about the results!

A professional PR person, who works mostly with fiction and nonfiction authors, had some advice for me as a poet that I'd like to share with you. NYT Bestseller M.J. Rose, author and founder of Authorbuzz.com, the first marketing company for authors, had some surprising advice for poets who are going to prepare to market a book. Try to get a single poem to be broadly seen or to "go viral." A great example of this is Maggie Smith's "Good Bones," a poem that got great buzz on Twitter and was read on the television show "Madam Secretary," which led to articles and greater name recognition. If you haven't read the poem, look it up!

M.J. Rose suggests:

No one can buy a book they have never heard of, so you need to get your poems seen. The market for poetry is small, but strong and it can tap into the gift market as well. The benefit you have over a novelist is that a poem is a complete unit and can be given away so people can get a sense of your work without it compromising the book. I think you should think of clever ways to present your poems. For instance—instead of just trying to get in poetry magazines or websites, find a topic in one of your poems and go after the audience of that topic. For instance, if you write poetry about nature—take the book to any and all nurseries and botanical gardens in your area and see if they will take five books on consignment for the gift shop. Find nature sites and give them a poem for free in exchange for a live link to your Amazon page. If you talk about politics in your poetry—try to get a local newspaper to use one on their website/in their paper. Poetry is contained—print up beautiful or powerful or thoughtful cards with your poem and a photo or drawing and give them out to people. Be as creative with where your poems can be seen as you are with your words.

I think this advice from M.J Rose is interesting—the idea of poem publicity as "gift!"

Action Items:

1. Write down one thing you can do to be part of a writing community in your area—whether it's volunteering, going to a reading series, or starting a writing group. Then, do it!

2. Extra credit/advanced. Write a "marketing plan" for your book, even if your book deal isn't quite solid yet. Draw up a strategic plan

for getting together a mailing list, figuring out your story and your selling points, and other practical, if unpoetic, ways to get your book into readers' hands.

3. Ask your publisher what you can do help out! Sometimes the publisher will have a ready-made handout for you; sometimes it'll start a useful conversation. Whatever you do, let your publisher know that you're willing to pitch in and help make your book a success!

4. Think about ways you might give a poem away in order to help spread the word about your work. Post one of the poems from your book on Twitter, or get a broadside printed to take to future readings or to give out to local businesses.

CHAPTER 8: GETTING INTO BOOKSTORES

About Distribution And Small Press Publishers

Whether you get into big chain bookstores, Amazon, or independent bookstores depends on your publisher and what kind of distribution they use. *Distribution* refers to the way they distribute their books to the market. The company that the publisher hires to do this is known as the *distributor.*

The primary distributors for small/medium poetry presses are Ingram, Small Press Distribution (SPD), and Consortium. Consortium makes publishers jump through lots of hoops, so only presses with significant time, money, and other resources have their distribution through them. All three of these distributors should make it simple to get your book into bookstores, however, some distributors refuse returns. This can mean bookstores will not carry your books.

Some small presses only distribute through their own websites and some don't use Amazon for ethical reasons. Both of these may impact your sales, but you don't have control over your publisher. When you decide on a publisher for your book, check their website or ask them about how they distribute their books. People can't buy your books in bookstores that aren't carrying your book. Fortunately, there are several ways to work around the distribution problems you can encounter with a small press publisher.

Consignment

Consigning usually entails signing a contract with a bookstore where they agree to carry your book for a certain percentage—usually, around 40-50 percent (and yes, that's painful, especially if your author discount is around 30-40 percent). But it's better than nothing. It is also up to you to provide the books to the bookstore. This is what happens to most small press poets when they want to do a bookstore reading and the store doesn't already carry their book for whatever reason. Most bookstores that consign your book will have you sign a contract, and they will keep track of your book sales. However, you also need to keep good records on where your books are consigned. I know from experience that most bookstores won't track you down to give you a check or return unsold books. You will also need to be patient. I've had to wait for over a year to get paid for consigned copies, even from prominent university bookstores.

Direct Marketing

Target stores you know and like. You can have some success contacting bookstores across the country yourself—offering a PR kit, a tip sheet, and even a print copy of your book in exchange for them considering carrying your book. This targeting is more likely to work for small independent bookstores. If you have a strong relationship with a local bookstore and you are a regular customer who buys a lot of books, approach them in person about carrying your book. Consider calling a former hometown bookstore where your name is familiar; you just need to pick up the phone.

Sandra Beasley, author of *Don't Kill the Birthday Girl: Tales from an Allergic Life* (published by Crown) and the poetry books, *Count the Waves* and *I Was the Jukebox,* (published by Norton) has some short tips for how to talk to your favorite bookstores, along with some of the information you should provide to them:

If you're getting ready to query bookstores for the first time in regards to readings, here is how I break it down...

- *Friendly opening relating your connection to the store (ideally, you have been there at least once) or the area.*

- *Brief description of your book: genre, theme, press, publication date. If it won a prize in tandem with publication, mention that.*

- *Platform for crowd draw. Do you have a nearby academic affiliation? Are you open to pairing with a local reader?*

- *Give a range of dates available for reading. Be sure to specify if you're available for weekends, weeknights, or both.*

- *Small JPG of your cover art; let them know both cover art and author photo are available in hi-res if needed.*

More extensive advice is shared by Kelly Davio, a poet, publicist, and essayist as well as the Founding Editor for *Tahoma Literary Review*. Here are her tips for connecting with your chosen bookstore representative:

- *Have a pitch ready. It's great if you can get on the phone with a bookstore's buyer. That's step one. But if you simply tell that buyer that you have a book and she should stock it, you haven't actually differentiated your book from anyone else's or created a compelling case for her to invest shelf space in your work. Before you cold call, try boiling your jacket copy down to a pithy few sentences, and be prepared to name a few comparable titles. Better still, have some thoughts ready about why your book is relevant in the current cultural climate.*

- *Market your book, not your achievements. I once met a woman who couldn't stop talking about the fact that she was once a Stegner fellow. She could only talk about her writing in relationship* to this long-ago honor in her life. "But what do you write?" I asked her. "Well, during The Stegner," she'd say, and she'd be off again. (I never did find out what kind of poems she wrote.) The thing is, nobody gives a flying leap about her Stegner decades later. There are new fellows, new writers doing new things and putting new books out. Is it great if you've had a big fellowship? Absolutely. But it's not a basis on which to market your book. (Honestly, can you really imagine walking into a bookshop and buying something just because the author was a former Stegner fellow?) Focus what you have to say on your work, not your accolades.

- Buyers need to know how the heck to get your book. So let's say your phone pitch went well, and you drummed up some interest. Now what's a conference organizer, for example, supposed to do to get copies of your book? If you're drawing a blank, that's a problem. You should know which distributor your publisher uses, and be ready to provide contact info. Or, you should be ready to provide consignment information. You should also have handy access to your ISBN number. (All the info we're talking about here, from pitch to comparable titles and distributor contact info to ISBN, is what your Tip Sheet is for, incidentally. Have one, send it out, and keep it in front of you when you're making calls.)

Bypass The Bookstore

While we all love to go into our neighborhood bookstore and see our work proudly displayed on the shelf, the best place to sell your book may not be a bookstore. Frankly, there is a lot of competition to get on the poetry shelf at bookstores as they are very worried, in the current economic climate, about their own profit margins. This issue can become even tougher to overcome if your publisher doesn't accept returns, which many small presses won't— again, no one wants to go under just to promote your book. However, there may be other ways to sell your book than traditional booksellers.

Consider Seattle-area poet Peter Pereira, who also happens to be a doctor. Peter sold an astounding number of his wonderful first poetry collection, *Saying the World* (Copper Canyon, 2003) at medical conferences where he gave talks about related medical issues. Attendees were so excited by Peter's presentations that they were eager to buy the book from him after his sessions.

For several years after its inception, I gave presentations at Seattle's GeekGirlCon about poetry and pop culture. After these talks, I would regularly sell books directly to those who heard me speak. I would get additional sales from the conference bookseller (The University of Washington Bookstore) through the duration of the Con.

Think about the types of events and activities you attend—which of these might be a good place to sell your book? Remember to focus on events that are in line with the themes of your book and what you are passionate about. Don't just be there to "hock your wares." Your passion will inspire your future readers to pick up your book in these situations.

Action Items:

1. Write down a list of your favorite bookstores, not just in your city but around the country (or even world, if you get ambitious.) From this list, choose the stores you want to contact when your book comes out. Research their contact information and find out if they provide details on their website for authors about consignment or book buying.

2. Walk in to your favorite local bookstore and talk to a manager about their process of buying books from local authors. If you're lucky, someone will get talk-y and give you even more tips! The first time doing this is the hardest. It will get easier!

CHAPTER 9: SWAG!

What Is Swag?

Swag refers to promotional materials given away by companies, publishers, or authors. The term "swag" comes historically from slang for "stolen goods" but more colloquially, "Stuff We All Get." These are the small things that you want in the hands of people who might be interested in buying your book. Swag can be passed out at readings, left at bookstores and cafes, sent to your mailing list, and given out as thank you gifts to those who purchase your book. People like to carry away a memento of a reading, even if they don't buy your book.

The most common poet swag includes book postcards, book business cards that show your cover image, and bookmarks. If you are lucky, your publisher will provide this for you. I've had some publishers spring for postcards and others make bookmarks, but some publishers don't offer to create swag. You can make more expensive swag, like t-shirts, mugs, pens, and toys—these aren't items most authors can afford to hand out for free. It's a good idea to check with your publisher and cover artist regarding copyright before you create swag using your book's cover art.

Designing Book Postcards

Sometimes your publisher will design a book postcard for you, and some will offer to mail them. If they don't offer to do this, it's not hard to create your own book-promoting postcards online. The most basic design for a book announcement postcard includes your book cover art on one side. The reverse side has information on how to order your book and a reserved space for the address and stamp.

You can ask your publisher for a full-color high-resolution version of the book cover (the higher the better). Online printers can handle most general image file formats, as long as the resolution is at least 300DPI. If the resolution is too low, the image will be blurry, and no one wants to pay for blurry cards.

I used this cover graphic from my publisher to create the following book card on the Vistaprint website:

Figure 3: RSD Postcard front

THE ROBOT SCIENTIST'S DAUGHTER

by

JEANNINE HALL GAILEY

Dazzling in its descriptions of a natural world imperiled by the hidden dangers of our nuclear past, this book presents a girl in search of the secrets of survival.

Jeannine Hall Gailey creates for us a world of radioactive wasps, cesium in the sunflowers, and robotic daughters. She conjures the intricate menace of the nuclear family and nuclear history, juxtaposing surreal cyborgs, mad scientists from fifties horror flicks and languid scenes of rural childhood.

Available March 2014 - $15.95
from Amazon or from...

Mayapple Press
www.mayapplepress.com
ISBN: 978-1936419425

Request a copy signed by the author at
www.webbish6.com/rsd

Scan for more information

Figure 4: Postcard back

Here are some tips for creating the back of your card:

- Pick a font that is legible and not too small.

- Pay attention to the space for postage. (It's in the top right).

- Leave room for the address label and any personal notes you might write. If you would like extra space for personal notes, consider a design that leaves the back of the card blank, which is shown below in Figure 5. If you don't leave room for a return address label, your postcard can't be returned (indicating that the recipient's address is no longer valid).

- The postal service often adds a strip at the bottom of postcards, so mail yourself a random postcard, and pay close attention to what gets marked and covered.

- Always keep up on the latest postage and card size requirements (check the USPS website), and use the minimum postage. Sadly, there is no forever stamp for postcards.

- Note that I included a QR code on the back of my postcard. This code is a machine-readable representation of the URL for this book on my website (I could have made it a link to the Amazon page or the product page on my publisher's website). Many people can read QR codes on their smartphones, so this is a good way to get potential buyers straight to your point-of-sale location. There are many websites and apps available to create a QR code. Search online for *QR code generator*.

Below is another example of a card from my third book which was created by my publisher. Note that both the information and the image are on the front of the card, leaving the entire backside free for postage, addresses (including return address), and handwritten notes.

Figure 5: Postcard with all book info on the front

Sending Out Postcards

As soon as your book is available for order or pre-order—send out your postcards! Send them to everyone on your mailing list. You can design a similar email announcement—with a graphic for your book cover and info on how to order it—and send it out to your e-mail list. These mailings are a serious tactic for book sales because your friends, family, family friends, and extended acquaintances will find out the specifics about your book's release and availability. And hopefully they will order it.

Business Cards

Most writers have their own business cards to exchange with people at poetry readings, writing conferences, and workshops—anywhere you might meet other writers and publishers with whom you want to remain in contact. Back in the day, I used to print my own cards on those perforated sheets of 10 cards using my inkjet, and later, laser printer, but now there are numerous online printers that make it easy to create high-quality business cards in bulk with good color graphics. I've used Vistaprint and MOO, but there are many others.

These online printing services, in addition to being affordable, have very easy online design tools that make it simple to create your card. They even allow you to print on both sides of the card. Since my first book came out, I have been designing my business cards with the book cover in color on the front side and print text in two-tone on the back. Each time I have a new book come out, I reprint my business card with the new book cover. By doing this, everyone who receives my card not only has my contact information, but also gets a reminder about my latest book. Non-writers, to whom I give my cards, seem to find this especially intriguing.

The following images are an example of the front and back of one of my business cards, created by MOO:

Figure 6: Front side with book cover art

Figure 7: This is the backside, which is 2-color

You can fit many types of information on a business card, but I usually include only my name, email address, website, and Twitter handle. Of course, you can add a professional title that you are especially proud of or your phone number. Make sure to always double and triple check this information before committing to print the order.

Business cards that display your cover image can also become swag as they make excellent magnets. Everyone loves magnets—your book cover on people's appliances. How cool is that? You can easily purchase self-adhesive magnets that stick onto a standard size business card. Stick the card to the magnet so that your book cover is displayed. Pass these magnets out at your readings or give them to people when they purchase your book. If you choose a non-standard size card (like MOO business cards) you may have to do some cutting in order for the card to fit on the magnet. I invested in a craft tool that attaches magnetic film to the back of my cards, but hey, I also own a laminator. Laminators are awesome, and you can purchase one for less than $30. I now laminate all kinds of things, including bookmarks and my book pricing cards.

Bookmarks

Bookmarks are classic swag. People love to take home a bookmark, and I often hand them out to people who are interested in my book but do not buy it at my readings. They then have a souvenir that will remind them about my book when they consider buying some new reading material. I laminate my bookmarks and also give them away to people who purchase my book. The following image is an example of how I position bookmarks (for two of my books) on a single page:

Figure 8: Bookmark layout for printing

Unlike business cards and postcards, online printers aren't set up specifically to create bookmarks. However, bookmarks are fairly easy to do yourself if you have some skill with word processing software, such as Word. Simply lay out your text and graphics in a 2x4 (2 rows, 4 columns) table using as much as possible of a standard 8.5"x11" page. You will be able to fit 8 bookmarks per sheet. Print the bookmarks on a heavyweight cardstock (your local print shop can give you options) and cut into individual bookmarks.

Other Types Of Swag

Cardstock-based swag is standard for any PR campaign. Depending on your book, you may come up with other kinds of swag to give away at readings and appearances. These various swag items should be fun and memorable, but also inexpensive. Here are some ideas for other types of swag:

- At the launch party for my first book, my publisher made cookies decorated with an image from the book cover.

- For *The Robot Scientist's Daughter*, I handed out little plastic robots and robot rings (I think these were cupcake toppers for kids' birthdays).

- A poet I know had pencils monogrammed with the title of his book.

- If you are friends with a printer or artist (or if your publisher creates broadsides), it would be fun to create your own broadside of one of your poems to give away as swag. One of my artist friends designed a broadside of my poem "The Snow Queen Explains" and I gave them away at holiday readings. If you have some basic design skills, this is something you can create yourself using word processing software. Print it at your local print shop.

Although this is more expensive, you can explore options for getting your book cover printed on everything from T-shirts and mousepads to tote bags and coffee mugs. Most online printers and web sites like CafePress and Vistaprint offer these options. I had several tote bags printed with some of my book covers using PictureItOnCanvas.com. They did a great job. However, these totes were part of a special offer and ended up being inexpensive. Remember to check with your publisher and cover artist regarding copyright before putting your book cover on swag.

Action Items:

1. Contact your publisher and ask for a high-resolution graphic of your book cover for use in promoting your book.

2. Find several online printers that make postcards and business cards and explore your various design options and costs.

3. Choose a printer and design a postcard or business card online using your book's cover art image and/or your author photo.

4. Create a list of different types of swag that would be useful in promoting your book. Think about traditional swag and also consider the unique themes in your book and how those could be turned into some unique swag. Research the various options and costs in terms of creating your specific swag ideas.

CHAPTER 10: I'M NOT TALKING ABOUT PLATFORMS, BUT. . .

Ways To Make Yourself Discoverable As A Writer

The idea of a "platform" sounds commercial and can be defined in many ways. In book marketing, it refers to *your presence in the world, online and in real time*. Your platform might include your website, your blog, your network of friends and associates, your social media networks, your public speaking engagements, media appearances, including radio and television, your newsletter, and your contribution to magazines. Your platform can be anything that defines you as a "brand" and extends your "reach"—that is, the number of people you affect, who might eventually purchase your book.

Remember in *Chapter 5: Preparing for Success* where I mentioned "building your platform?" Well, now that your book is out, use that platform to announce your publication news—not 100 times an hour as that will only annoy people. It's good to talk about your newly-published book on your blog, post a picture of your cover or a reading event on Facebook, or send out info on your book launch on Twitter. You might consider posting a personal essay that is related to your book's topic. Maybe mention your book in an interview or write a pitch letter or send out a PR release to your local newspaper. The people who follow you, who are friends with you, are certainly interested in what you have to say and in your new book.

Defining The "Brand Called You"

What makes up a platform? Who are you? How do you define yourself? How can people find you or find out more about you? In addition to being a poet, are you also a gamer, an instructor, a quilter, a member of a rock band? What can you share with a specific community that will attract a following? In the late 1990s, I sat in a dark room listening to a seminar for "knowledge workers" by an enthusiastic up-and-comer in the business world who talked about making yourself distinct from the masses, creating "the brand called you." I heard this phrase and it stuck in my mind. I recommend that you read an article that is now a classic in advertising, journalism, and marketing—"A Brand Called You" by Tom Peters in *Fast Company*. There is a link to this article at the end of the book.

To maximize the strength of your platform, you should consistently brand yourself across all websites, social media, blogs, and even your email. Ideally, the name you use for your website, email, and social media accounts (also known as your handle or username) should be your name or some recognizable form of your name. In this way, you are always using your name when promoting your work.

The exception to this rule, which I've claimed for myself, is if you have a well-known nickname that you have previously used across your social media platforms. In 2005 when I started my blog, I chose "webbish6" as my domain name (which came from my techy days—long story, but it involved a VP asking my team to make a website more "webbish6"). Because I used this nickname, I have consistently used "webbish6" on other social media accounts, including my Twitter handle. (I also registered the domain jeanninegailey.com, which is an alias for my webbish6.com domain, so that I can provide more authoritative looking links to my site.) You can ask your website host about creating domain aliases. Whether you decide to use your own name or a well-known pseudo name, you should use it consistently across your platform accounts.

A Professional Website

As I mentioned earlier, having a professional website is absolutely essential at this point in your writing career. Not just a website for your book, but a website for you, and for your next book, too. It's tempting to create a website based on the name of your book. However, if you do this, you will find yourself creating and hosting a second website when your next book comes out. If you want to register a domain name for your book, you can use the title as a domain "alias," which can be redirected to your main website. Your web hosting company will be able to help you do this.

Your website should include these basics: a bio, a headshot, a way to contact you, links to your work, links to buy your book. The site should have a clean and functional design so that it looks current and contemporary. I've found it helpful to enlist the assistance of tech-savvy friends and family in building my website. I am fortunate to know people who are web developers and graphic designers, so they are skilled with tools, such as Adobe Illustrator. If you know individuals who are tech-savvy, offer them payment or at least a dozen homemade chocolate chip cookies in exchange for their trouble. It will be worth it to have a professional, recognizable website.

If you don't have tech-savvy friends and don't want to spend professional design dollars, there are many services that will help you "do-it-yourself" (DIY). Many web hosts provide visual tools that make it easy to get a site up and running all by yourself. You just select themes and drag-and-drop images and components to refine the basic site design. Weebly and Wix are two services that you can use to design a site for free. Other hosting services, like iPage.com, will register your domain for free and provide rich design tools with low hosting costs.

In addition, hosted blogging services like Wordpress and Blogger will provide a free blogging site as a subdomain ("yourblog.wordpress.com"), and you can post static pages. This way, you can also post pages to help promote your book along with your blog. The drawback to these sites is that your brand is limited to the subdomain—you don't get your own URL. I talk more about blogging in *Chapter 12: Social Media and Blogs*.

Even if you DIY your site or enlist friends to help, the whole enterprise can still cost you some money— hosting, website registration, design, and other fees. Remember, being a published author is a professional career, and this is an official business expense, which you may be able to write off on your taxes against your writing earnings. (Check with an accountant or tax consultant.)

Be Searchable

The internet is a vast labyrinth of data—how will potential readers find you or your book? Of course they search for you and your work using Google, Bing, Yahoo, or one of the dozens of other search engines out there. Most people don't go past the first page or two of search results, so it's important to pay attention to "search engine optimization"

(SEO) when authoring your site's content. You don't need to be an SEO expert—and you likely aren't going to show up in searches for "awesome poet." However, you do want your name, book title, and website to come up first when people type your name into Google.

How do you do that? Well, starting up your website, as I mentioned above, will help. Filling your website with useful content (that people want to link to) is another plus. Once your website has regular visitors, consider beginning a blog and connecting with other poetry/book bloggers to see if they can assist in getting your book reviewed or mentioned. Some of this you can control, and some you can't. Obviously, you want positive mentions about you and your book. (And if, like a friend of mine, you have the problem of having the same name as a semi-famous porn star, well, you're just going to have to fight porn with poetry. You'd be surprised who is at the top of that Google search now—it's not the porn star!)

When writing for SEO, you need to pay close attention to what are known as "keywords," which are simply words or phrases that people are searching for. Using keywords that are too generic, like "poems" or "haiku," won't help because they are too general. You also want to avoid keywords that are too specific because few people will be searching for them. The main keywords for you to use are your full name and the full title of your book. You may also want other keywords depending on the subject of your book. Good keywords for posts discussing my fourth book *The Robot Scientist's Daughter* might include terms like: "Oak Ridge," "nuclear," and "secret city."

For Techy Poets

Since most writers build their author websites through a website creation service (like iPage or Wix), check the help section to make changes to your site in order to optimize your search results. You can also contact customer support or ask a tech-savvy friend to help you.

If you are familiar with HTML formatting language, then you can implement the following suggestions directly on your website. The SEO rules are constantly being tweaked by the providers, but some basic tips include:

- When building your author website, choose the best domain name, title and description. Google builds its search results using the first 60 or so characters in the page title (which is not on the page body but in the header) and the first 150 or so characters in the first paragraph. You need to make these clear and get as many keywords in there as possible.

- Pay attention to headings. There should only be one H1 heading on your page (not to be confused with the page title), and it should convey exactly what the page or post is about. Headings are given more weight in searches, so have good headings (H1-H4).

- Know your keywords. Use your whole name and book name in your blog posts and pages. If there are other keywords that define your book (in the case of my first book "pop-culture" or "superhero") those should also appear near the top of the page. There are tools that you can use to analyze your keywords.

- Try to focus on a single theme in a given page or post. I'm personally not great at this, but it provides a more concise set of keywords in the page.

- Use links and ask people to link to your site. In the early days of blogging, the "blog roll" was a great way to build SEO in the poetry blog community.

Research SEO online to find out more information.

Speaking Or Teaching

I've focused a lot on the website, but there are other components to your platform. Consider your in-person appearances as part of your platform. Even if you're not a teacher, speaker, or workshop leader by profession, this is a great time to seek out gigs speaking to colleges and even high school classes, teaching workshops in local literary centers, and generally interacting with the public. Why? It increases your profile and your exposure as an expert in your field. Plus, you're helping others find the joy in poetry, which is a noble cause in and of itself.

Writing

Think about writing a personal essay or op-ed about subject matter related to your book. Be open to doing interviews about subject matter related to your book. If you have friends who blog about books, offer to write a "guest blog post" on a topic related to your book.

As poets, we must also write "non-poetry" to attract non-poets to our writing—this expands our audience. If you write about sailing, find sailing websites or magazines that might be interested in your first person essay on sailing (mention your book, of course.)

Social Media

Yes, social media is part of building a platform, but I think it is complicated enough to deserve its own chapter. We will discuss social media in detail in *Chapter 12: Social Media and Blogs*.

Action Items:

1. Write down one practical thing you can do to build your writing platform. Have you created a website? Started a blog? Joined Twitter and followed your favorite writers? Joined Facebook and created an author page?

2. Google yourself and also the name of your book. If your website doesn't come up, ask what you (and your publisher) can do to make sure the links that come up are relevant.

3. Talk to someone in your local community about making an appearance, whether it be in a church, a community center, a school, or a bookstore. It's good practice and it gives you and opportunity to interact with others— always good for introverts. It's a win-win— others get poetry, you get to feel good about being out there talking about poetry.

CHAPTER 11: INTERVIEWS WITH POETS WHO ARE PLATFORM EXPERTS

Using Platforms To Promote Books

Now that you have a better idea of what platforms are and how they can be used to promote your poetry book, let's hear from two experts on platforms, Sandra Beasley and Robert Lee Brewer.

Interview With Sandra Beasley

Sandra Beasley is author of three poetry collections: *Count the Waves*; *I Was the Jukebox*, winner of the Barnard Women Poets Prize; and *Theories of Falling*, winner of the New Issues Poetry Prize. She is also the author of the memoir *Don't Kill the Birthday Girl: Tales from an Allergic Life*. Sandra has demonstrated expertise at promoting her poetry and has experienced a traditional PR campaign for her memoir from a major publisher.

What are your top tips for developing a platform for book publicity?

So much of this publicity stuff is trial and error and the power of organic relationships. You can't fake it, or rush it. But here's a couple of things that make a big difference for me:

There will be time-sensitive opportunities that come your way, where you may be one of several invited to take part, and whoever responds the quickest will be chosen. Always respond to requests for PR information in a timely and consistent manner. So have a folder on your computer that is a go-to publicity kit, containing:

- 50-word bio note, 100-word bio note, 250-word bio note.

- List of recent readings.

- List of recent outreach events (classroom visits, panels, radio) and go-to topics for discussion.

- Hi-res JPG of book cover and hi-res JPG of author photo in color.

- Hi-res JPG of author photo in grayscale.

Make sure the filenames for all of these are clear and relevant to an outside user.

What else can authors do to increase their "reach?"

Pick 3-4 literary journals that published poems from your collection and are based (or have poetry editors based) within a 90-minute driving radius. Write a nice, short note to the editor reintroducing yourself and the book, saying how thrilled you were to be in the journal, and asking if he or she can make an intro to a nearby reading series or bookstore. If it clicks, and you schedule a reading, be sure it's at a time when that editor can attend and hang out.

Help increase the chance of your book being taught—spread the word, through social media or a personal website, that you will offer a 30-45 minute Skype session to any class that has purchased the book as a text. Make a video-poem and upload it to YouTube, which can be done on your own time (for me, that means middle of the night) using stock photography, or partner with a local artist who is excited to handle the visual elements. Design a writing prompt based on a recurring thematic or stylistic element in your poems; create a handout that puts one of your poems in the context of 3-4 canonical influences.

Maybe that'll all seem a bit self-important, but it has worked for me. I hope it is helpful to others. Congrats to everyone with a book on its way!

Interview With Robert Lee Brewer

Robert Lee Brewer is a hardworking individual, editing everything from his *Writer's Digest* blog posts to *Poet's Market* and *Writer's Market*. He also hosts a regular "platform challenge" for writers.

Brewer is Senior Content Editor of the *Writer's Digest Writing Community*, which means he helps writers through several channels, including posting on the *Poetic Asides* and *There Are No Rules* WritersDigest.com blogs, editing *WritersMarket.com* and its free weekly e-newsletter, editing the *Writer's Market* and *Poet's Market* books, giving online webinars and tutorials, judging poetry contests, writing a poetry column in *Writer's Digest* magazine, and much more. He's also the author of *Solving the World's Problems*. Follow him on Twitter @RobertLeeBrewer.

So many writers are freaked out by the word "platform," maybe because it sounds too "business-y" or it's overwhelming to think about having a platform. How would you explain what a platform is to a writer new to this idea?

Platform is the quantifiable reach authors have to their target audience. So, it could be followers on social media sites, subscribers to a newsletter or e-mail list, unique visitors to a blog, number of people who subscribe to a publication in which an author has a regular column, and so on. The idea is that authors have a better chance at selling more books if they have a bigger platform.

Of course, it can be misleading to think of it as merely a "numbers" game, because I would argue that 100 people who are willingly on a personal e-mail list are more valuable for selling books than 1,000 followers on Twitter. That's because they're more engaged.

If a poet has limited time, what parts of their platform do you think are the most important for them to focus on? Someone asked me recently at a class I was guest-teaching how many hours I spent weekly or monthly on online book promotion and platform work, and I couldn't really estimate, as it has become so ingrained in my routine (blogging, Facebook, Twitter, website work, sending out submissions and queries) which is really a little scary!

If a poet truly has limited time, I would argue that the poetry should come first. This is true, whether we're talking platform or submitting to publications. That said, if poets don't carve out a little time for submitting and platform, their work is likely to collect dust and never connect with readers. So what's the most important for poets to focus upon?

It's different for each person, but I think everyone can benefit from getting on some low impact social media sites like Facebook and Twitter. If used appropriately, poets can connect with other poets, publishers, and publications. It's an easy way to make connections without a lot of commitment on the part of the poet.

After that, submitting work is probably the most important. Publication does two things for a poet: First, it puts a stamp of approval on the work from an objective editor; second, it helps the poet reach readers.

Having a website is important, because it's a centralized piece of online real estate for an author that readers can turn to even as other platforms rise and fall.

Beyond that, I just encourage folks to try various things (blogging, podcasting, various social media sites, live events) to find what works for them. What works for one poet might not work for another. So there are best practices, but there's also trial and error and experimentation.

Why do you provide space and encourage a platform challenge for writers? What are you hoping to help writers accomplish?

One of the cool things about my job is that I get to help writers achieve more success. I write articles, edit books, post on blogs, and so on, sure, but the main thing I do is help writers achieve more success. If I'm doing my job, then I expect writers to find success and want to build on that success by subscribing to the magazine, taking online courses, and buying books.

In regards to the platform challenge, I'm hoping to help writers challenge themselves to work at their writing platform with easy daily tasks that show what writers can do. And hopefully, they build upon that after the October challenge is over, and I'll find out about various success stories for months and years after. That's been my experience with other challenges I've hosted, whether they're for building a writer platform or writing poetry. And success stories always blow me away and inspire me to do more.

How do think poets in particular can help increase their "reach" by developing their platform? What would you say has been most surprising for you in terms of growing your poetry audiences?

I think blogging has really helped me. Social media sites have helped. Speaking at live events has helped too. As far as selling books, I've found that publishing new poems helps sell the old book.

It's not a surprise anymore, but I think one thing I've learned as an author and through working in publishing is that numbers are helpful—but they don't tell the whole story. An engaged audience that comments on a blog is more powerful than a bunch of "fans" on Facebook; an engaged email list that buys new books is more valuable than a gazillion followers on Twitter. It's not that a gazillion followers on Twitter is not valuable in its own right, but it's a matter of how engaged the audience is.

Your job is pretty demanding, and yet you find time to devote to your own writing and promoting your latest book projects. How do you find that balance?

I prioritize. I've never seen an episode of *Breaking*

Bad, Game of Thrones, NCIS, How I Met Your Mother, etc. I've only seen parts of a few episodes of *The Big Bang Theory* and *The Walking Dead* while visiting other people's homes. I haven't really played video games since my Game Boy (the big, clunky one with the green screen) died years ago. It's not that I have anything against watching TV or playing video games, but I have five kids in two states and volunteer with my church and Cub Scouts—so I have to draw the line somewhere.

And when I feel the urge to write a poem or sketch out an idea, I stop what I'm doing and write, because I know that if I don't, I'll be distracted (thinking about what I could be writing). Might as well get it out of my system and then get back to the task at hand.

So at times, I guess, it's not really balancing as much as throwing myself into whatever it is that I'm doing. It's often not that balanced, but I've learned that's okay.

CHAPTER 12: SOCIAL MEDIA AND BLOGS

Promote Your Work In Your PJs

One of the more recent and potentially invaluable parts of book promotion is the use of social media. Some poets hate these online services with a passion and want no part of it, while others use Twitter and Facebook with enjoyment and ease. Participating in some variety of social media will allow you to connect with readers you might not reach in other ways. It also lets you connect with readers in other parts of the country and around the world, something that was previously impossible without travel.

Today, there are many ways to connect on social media, so you should be able to find a service that is right for you, and I recommend using more than one. If you're a visual type of person, consider posting pictures of your book or poems on Instagram or Pinterest. Facebook has become a good way to connect with the over-40 crowd, while Twitter is better for connecting to the under-40 crowd. Goodreads and LibraryThing target avid readers and amateur book reviewers. Most social media outlets have dedicated apps so that you can interact with your audience from your phone whenever you have spare time.

In almost any of these social media sites, you will find dedicated spaces for writers and readers. Facebook has community pages and groups just for poets. The Twitter hashtag *#poetparty* is used for a monthly poetry discussion online.

Blogs, one of the original ways of creating an audience online, are my favorite way to interact with readers. Blogs emphasize "long-form" sharing—they draw readers in by letting you write about your day, maybe post a picture, AND talk about something going on in the literary world. Incidentally, you can follow my blog at webbish6.com. Here are some other poetry blogs: January Gill O'Neil's Poet Mom: poetmom.blogspot.com, Mary Biddinger's The Word Cage: wordcage.blogspot.com, Charles Jensen's Kinemapoetics: charles-jensen.com//kinemapoetics-blog, The Poetry Foundation's *Harriet*: www.poetryfoundation.org/harriet.

Remember to build a following by offering a stream of good and interesting content to your followers. If you plan to only use social media to promote your book, you probably won't be successful. When using social media to promote your book, you need to decide what's best for you in terms of time investment, and how you best communicate. Are you verbal? Do you think in pictures? Long-form (blog post) or short (tweet)? Target the outlets you like best or will best reach your readers. Offer poetry fans something of interest, or they won't have a reason to follow you—no one wants to consume a steady stream of PR. This chapter provides a summary of the major social media outlets and how they can best be used to promote your book.

Choose Your Username Wisely

As I mentioned earlier, you should always use the same username/handle across all social media platforms. This helps to maximize the strength of your platform. And, your username should be your name or some consistent form of your name. In this way, you are always using your name when promoting your work.

Here is something to keep in mind—your social media accounts are the public persona of your professional career. As such, you must be careful about what you post from your "official" accounts. This is especially important when you are applying for jobs, like tenure-track professor, high school teacher, a position in the corporate world, or any professional employment. If you want to mess around with friends, post embarrassing selfies, or make "bold statements" that might not be taken well by most of your audience, you should create separate social media accounts to do that. Always remember, even with privacy settings, you should consider everything posted on social media as public, so if there's something you don't want the entire world to know, maybe refrain from posting it online. Employers often review the social media accounts of potential hires.

Facebook

Facebook is one of the largest social media sites with close to two billion global users as of this writing. Facebook lets you "friend" other users, then your friends will ostensibly see the items you post to your Facebook timeline. You can "like" other people's posts, share posts on your timeline, post your own pictures, and stream video. Many of your readers are probably already on Facebook—you just need to find them. This is a good place to create large networks of family and friends, the very people most interested in your books. There are two types of accounts on Facebook, a personal account that limits you to 5000 "friends" or a "Page", which is an account allowing you to have unlimited "Likes." You should consider starting with a personal account then create an author page using your real name, which is dedicated only to writing or poetry-related posts, events, and information.

You can create a page for your poetry book on Facebook. Here is my page for *The Robot Scientist's Daughter:* facebook.com/robotscientistsdaughter/. Friends can then like your book page, which helps you target promoting your book to users who are interested.

You can pay Facebook to promote (or "boost") your posts or author/book pages. Some poets have reported success when they target a specific interest group in their "boost," but I've personally not had stellar results. It doesn't cost much to try this out.

Pros: It's easy to share PR items and other news about your book with many people at a time. You can build pages for your author persona and separate pages specifically to market your book. Many poets are active on Facebook, and it's very easy to build a network there.

Cons: Facebook is designed to keep you engaged, so you may end up spending valuable writing time online.

Tip: Always post your PR items to your personal feed and your book/author pages' feeds, but stagger the posting by a day or two.

Twitter

Twitter is a messaging service that allows you to send 280-character messages (tweets), along with text and links, to people who follow you. Some people have thousands of Twitter followers and find themselves inspired to great wit and brevity because of that 280-character limit. On Twitter, you send info and links to a potentially large group of followers, and you can also direct message.

Twitter pioneered using the at (@) and hashtag (#) characters. For example, to mention me in a tweet, include @webbish6. To tweet to me directly, reply or start your tweet with @webbish6. Hashtags add an index to help people find your tweet by filtering discussions. The hashtag #poetparty is used for the monthly poetry discussion that I frequently take part in. If you search twitter for #poetparty, you will see previous discussions. You can also follow your favorite publishers and literary magazines on Twitter.

Be sure to interact with others on a regular basis. Retweet and favorite a few posts each day, if possible. Follow people whose writing you admire— you'd be surprised which writers are on Twitter (Margaret Atwood? Kaveh Akbar? Eve Ewing? Yup!). The more you use the platform, the more followers you will accumulate.

Note that tweets are very transient in nature, so it's easy for people to miss PR tweets about your book. The use of good and popular hashtags can make tweets a little easier to find. Ideally, you want your tweets to be retweeted. You will probably need to tweet the same item a few different times to reach all of your followers. Just don't get obnoxious with the number and frequency of similar tweets, or followers will mute you or unfollow you.

Pros: You can quickly and easily post links and pictures to lots of people. You don't have to follow people who choose to follow you, although this is often a good idea.

Cons: Tweets are very transient and often get missed. People can mute you without you knowing it. You might lose followers if you aren't very active on the platform or if you send out tweets that your followers aren't interested in.

Tip: Stay as active on Twitter as you can. People who frequently send out well-focused and interesting tweets tend to amass and keep followers.

LinkedIn

At first I resisted joining LinkedIn, as I thought it was merely for corporate business types. (Not that there's anything wrong with corporate business types—I was one for fifteen years!) I've found new readers and friends, and I've reconnected with old friends through LinkedIn—individuals I wouldn't have found on other social media platforms.

LinkedIn is popular with business people and can

also be used to link to your blog. It can help you make connections to other teachers, writers, and editors.

Pros: LinkedIn can help you connect to professionals in your field, which can be very valuable when you are also looking for professional employment. This is a great way to stay connected to current and former co-workers.

Cons: Since this is a professionally-focused network, people you connect with may not be as interested in poetry as those in other social networks and may not be as interested in buying your book.

Tip: Use your professional headshot in your LinkedIn profile. Don't saturate this channel with book announcements.

Goodreads And LibraryThing

Goodreads and LibraryThing are devoted especially to people who love books, which makes them great online places to hang out with others who enjoy reading. Readers can share what books they are reading or are planning to read. Both services encourage members to rate and publish reviews of the books they have read, which is another great thing about these services.

You should definitely join Goodreads or LibraryThing (ideally both) and set up an author page on the site(s) with your info and links to your website. You can watch people's reviews of your book as they arrive in real time.

Pros: These sites are full of people sharing what they are reading and also writing book reviews—what's not to love?

Cons: Not all reviewers appreciate poetry and many reviews are blunt and honest. If they don't like your book (or poetry in general), you will hear about it.

Tip: Set up giveaways—Goodreads will walk you or your publisher through this process, which is easy, and it creates excitement for your book. After your giveaway, when you are mailing out copies of your book, ask the winners if they would post a review.

Instagram

On Instagram you can follow other poets or post parts of your poems. Some poets have made entire careers from this alone, such as Rupi Kauer. On Instagram, the more hashtags, the better. Poets and poetry readers need to find you, so post hashtags such as #poetsofinstagram #poem #poetrybooks, etc. so that your photos can be found. *Forbes* referenced active book reviewers on Instagram as

"Bookstagrammers."

Pros: Instagram is great way to share your poems or even your PR materials. You can connect Instagram to both Facebook and Twitter so that your Instagram posts will automatically get posted to your other social networks.

Cons: You need to post compelling images to get noticed on Instagram. If you're great at composition and photos, and think visually, this is for you!

Tip: Post images of book covers and book parties, related art, or inspiring pieces. Hashtag relevant topics or groups you belong to.

Tumblr

Tumblr is a "micro-blogging" social media site where there is often less text and more media. Text posts are usually quite short, often sharing other people's posts combined with graphics or art. (Sort of like Facebook, but without the distractions.) Pictures frequently substitute for text, and I've seen many snapshots of poetry book pages. Poetry fans on Tumblr use it to post poems that they like. Many of my poems have shown up on Tumblr, even though I don't actively use it. Posters will usually include your name, so you can see which poem is being posted. When someone likes a post, they "reblog" the post—giving credit to the original poster. The more reblogs, the more popular the post. Note that "reposting" is frowned upon because it doesn't give credit to the original poster. Tumblr has a younger audience who actively reblogs content they are interested in. This is a great way to have your work shared with a younger audience.

My favorite Tumblr post is one that features a poem from my first book, *Becoming the Villainess*, combined with some fanfiction and an image from *The Vampire Diaries* TV show. It might technically be copyright infringement, but at least it's entertaining!

Pros: This is a great platform if you don't have the time to keep up a regular blog. It's also very easy to share and like posts.

Cons: Tumblr has a tightknit community, so it may be difficult to leverage for PR.

Tip: You can create an account to see if your poems are being "tumbled" by searching your name or book title in the Tumblr search engine.

Websites And Blogs

While you may not consider your personal website or blog a "social media" outlet, most blogs provide a mechanism to share links with blog readers. You can also easily share blog post links via LinkedIn, Facebook, and Twitter, which means your blog posts can do double-duty. This is my favorite form of social media and the one I've been at the longest—I started my blog in 2005, when there were only a few active poetry bloggers (*po-bloggers*). My current blog can be found at webbish6.com (also jeanninegailey.com). This blog, which is a WordPress site that I host myself, is also the main landing page for my website. It still has a "blogroll" on the side— which is a bunch of links to other poet and artist blogs (a tradition of blogs back in the day).

While I pay to host my own WordPress site, you can use WordPress or Blogger to host your blog for free, as long are you okay with your site being a subdomain that ends in *.blogger.com* or *.wordpress.com*, such as yourname.wordpress.com. Whatever way you to decide to go, you can make your site elaborate and beautiful, or keep it minimal.

I like blogging because it falls into the natural mode for writers and it's a regular form of journaling that can be good for your writing muscles when you're not writing anything else.

Be sure to post on a regular basis—this will help you build a regular audience. Post links to other useful content and to other people. Interact with people who comment on your blog. Such actions are called "engaging" with your audience!

Scheduling Posts

Studies have shown that there are certain times of day when it's best to post your blog entries. I think Tuesday and Thursday mornings are best. This, of course, will vary depending on the audience. Most blogging platforms let you schedule the time when your posts are published.

You can even keep the steady stream of posts on social media going when you are too busy to post. While I don't personally work this way, I have friends who are adamant about scheduling their work into chunks of time. Yet, they still want a steady stream of posts throughout the day or week while working on creative or other tasks. Services like Buffer and Hootsuite let you manage your social media platform by allowing you to write your posts and schedule the delivery of posts to your various social channels.

Action Items:

1. Sign up for at least one social media form that you're not already on and familiar with. Try it out for a few weeks. If you hate it, move on, but if you love it, it's a new way to get the word out about your book.

2. Try the following: post one thing a week on Facebook and Twitter about your book—a review, a blurb, your book cover, something exciting that's going on, or a book event that you have scheduled. Small enticing details about your book launch can make things more exciting for your fans! Add graphics to your posts to get more attention.

CHAPTER 13: INTERVIEWS WITH SOCIAL MEDIA EXPERTS

Poets Who Are Social Media Experts

Now that you have an idea of the social media landscape, let's hear from two poets who have been effectively using social media to promote their work—Collin Kelley and Killian Czuba.

Interview With Collin Kelley

Collin Kelley is the author of *The Venus Trilogy* of novels—*Conquering Venus*, *Remain in Light* and the forthcoming *Leaving Paris*. His poetry collections include *Render*, *Better To Travel*, *Slow To Burn* and *After the Poison*. I've been an admirer of Collin's work for some time (it doesn't hurt that we watch the same television shows and both write persona poetry!) and really admire the way he was an early adopter of platforms like Twitter and Facebook to promote his work.

Could you talk a little bit about how you got started with blogging and social media?

I started blogging back in 2003 just as blogs were becoming all the rage. This was before MySpace, Facebook, and Twitter. I had a static website before that, but once I started blogging all the traffic started going there, so I dumped the site and made my Modern Confessional blog my main "hub" on the Internet. I was an early adopter of MySpace, Facebook, and Twitter, and they all felt like a natural progression from blogging. The blog is still there and updated regularly but Facebook and Twitter are really where I interact the most these days. It doesn't hurt that I'm a big computer nerd and Internet addict either.

What has been the most effective way of getting the word out about your own books (poetry and fiction)? Do you notice a sales bump from online reviews, blog tours, and tweeting?

I think a good example is when I posted the sample chapters from my novel, *Remain in Light*. I posted the pages at Scribd. (another great site for writers to share their work) and then linked it around to Facebook, Twitter, Goodreads and my blog. In 24 hours, more than 100 people had read the chapters, and since then hundreds more have read them. Social media drove readers to the chapters and will, hopefully, make for good sales when the book is out later this year. Since I'm poor, most of my promotion for the previous novel and poetry collection was online. Without social media, there wouldn't have been nearly as many readers or sales.

What advice would you give a nervous poet about

getting on-board with Twitter, blogs, and Facebook?

Don't be frightened of it and start slowly. I guest lecture and lead classes now on social media for writers and the most asked question is "What do I do once I'm on Twitter and Facebook?" I highly recommend setting up a Facebook page for your book, so that you can be more direct in your promotion and sales, but you don't want to "hard sell" your book. The goal is to build community, so help other writers promote their books, find topics that relate to your books and interests, post funny YouTube clips—you're selling yourself as much as the book, and readers want to get to know authors, so let them into your world a bit. If you go on Facebook and just say over and over again, "Buy My Book," it's going to turn people off. The same applies to Twitter. If you want more followers on Twitter, become a source for good links and information, retweet links and information from your followers, and let your interests and personality shine through. Cultivating and building community on social media sites takes time, so work on it daily, but don't go crazy. Time management is the key. Spend a half hour each day updating your social media then get on with the actual writing.

Just out of curiosity: poetry blogs—are they over or not over? Why?

I don't think poetry blogs are through just yet, but

you'll notice more and more that poets are setting up their blog posts to link on Facebook and Twitter. That helps drive more traffic. I've seen a big drop in traffic at my blog over the last year, while the number of people following me and engaging at Facebook and Twitter continues to soar. There are some great poetry bloggers out there—C. Dale Young, Nic Sebastian, Kelli Russell Agodon, January O'Neil, Charles Jensen, Jessie Carty, Barbara Jane Reyes, and a certain Jeannine Hall Gailey all come to mind. There is always going to be a place on the web for more in depth writing and niche interests, so blogs will survive because of that. But faster and quicker ways to communicate, like Facebook, Twitter and whatever is being dreamed up by some teenager in his dorm room right now, are where the action is now.

You and Deb Ager have been running the "Poet Party" on Sundays on Twitter. How did that come together, and what do you think it's accomplishing? I really love to see the connections formed between poets who might not have met otherwise. It's also great getting advice on things (like Facebook pages for a new book!) in 240 characters or less.

Deb created the #poetparty (just follow the hashtag, as they say in Twitter-speak) last fall and it took off quickly. She asked me to co-host early on and we've built a solid following on Sunday nights. Introducing poets to each other, sharing links for submissions, contests, and poetry online is the real success of the #poetparty. While the event only lasts an hour (9 to 10 p.m. ET), we've noticed that poets continue to comment and share info throughout the week using the hashtag. It's taken on a life of its own. It's a very supportive group of poets who show up every Sunday night and we welcome poets of all stripes to join us. I also think the #poetparty is proof-positive that you can have active discussion, debate and community building on Twitter in real-time.

Interview With Killian Czuba

Killian Czuba is a fiction writer, comics enthusiast, podcaster, and social media/PR gun-for-hire. She is also full of infectious energy and enthusiasm. Check out both of her websites: killianczuba.com and scoutlitpub.tumblr.com. You can also follow her on Twitter @ScoutLitPub and @killianczuba.

How would you say most authors are using social media today, and how should they be using social media to be more effective at book promotion?

Not enough authors use social media. Many of them who I know personally admit to being afraid of it; they are daunted by a lack of knowledge about certain platforms, or the assumption of overwhelming time commitment. Now, some more famous authors do use it, to different degrees, and there are a few who really stand out to me (I'll use Twitter as my base example here): journalists Laura Hudson (@laura_hudson) and Ta-Nehisi Coates (@tanehisicoates), horror writer Joe Hill (@joe_hill), and lit fiction author Colson Whitehead (@colsonwhitehead). I gravitate towards following people who interact very personally and positively with their followers. I could follow X author, but they only tweet promotions or very removed and boring updates, so I don't. I could follow Y author, but they spend most of their time saying inflammatory things and fighting with people, so I don't.

Honestly, I think that the prose and poetry communities should take note of what the comics community is like. They are supportive, close-knit, and very friendly towards outsiders. They retweet fan photos and favorite enthusiastic tweets. They engage in conversation. Everyone gets political sometimes (and, believe me, that is necessary at times), but the overall feeling is one of improving the field, of adapting, of promoting the youngsters and new faces instead of sneering. I think authors need to embrace that supportive and socially engaged aspect to social media. That's the point, right? To be social. Check out someone like Kelly Sue DeConnick (@KellySue).

When people who I respect and admire on social media write a book, or suggest a book, I am far more likely to put it on my to-read list. My most recent example of this is my recent following of Caitlin Doughty (@thegooddeath) and my desire to read her new nonfiction book, *Smoke Gets in Your Eyes: And Other Lessons from the Crematory*. I think she's smart, and I like her as a person. That second part? That's all social media.

So, okay, summary: Get on Twitter. See how the people you like use it (because tastes vary, and that's part of the fun). Use it like they do.

This could be a loaded question—What is the best and most useful social media platform for promoting books right now, in your opinion? I know I've felt overwhelmed by the options (Tumblr, Instagram, Pinterest, Twitter, Facebook) and just haven't known where to spend my time. (Plus, as may be obvious, I love my long-form blogging!)

I think a combination of platforms is the way to go, but if you are crunched for time and only give yourself one new platform to master, then the answer is to focus on what each platform is good for, and pick that which will appeal to your audience. Doing YA? Go for Instagram. Have a 45yo+ general audience? Facebook. Funny, I know, but the internet changes quickly. Facebook is a great place to be, but it's not where the teenagers hang out anymore. If you have a broad age range OR a very niche community, use Tumblr and Twitter, and utilize tags. When in doubt, you should have a blog, too. Tumblr can fill that void, or WordPress, Blogger, etc—but a blog is best when paired with something more interactive (that way you seem like a person who actually cares about engaging, and not just talking). Whichever you pick, be present. There's a delicate line between consistent updating and spamming—everyone has a different tolerance, because life just can't be easy—but it is so important to post multiple times a week (even better? Tweet 3x a day, and fave a few other tweets).

What's the number one thing you see authors doing that you're like: "Please, just stop!"

Authors being vitriolic towards one another for petty reasons. There are legitimate reasons to criticize and demand action—some of which have been very prevalent recently—and then there are people who say "X people can't write," or "God, I hate Y because they're so successful." Am I envious of Eleanor Catton for writing a perfect Victorian Detective Mystery and winning the Booker for it? Yeah, but because her work is so good—NOT because she wrote it in her twenties. I could be resentful of her success, or give in to the feeling that I need to catch up, but instead I choose to admire it and share my appreciation of it. It's not just good karma, it makes the writing life feel more like an act of love than a competition to get into Harvard. (...Yes, I have been Netflix-marathoning Gilmore Girls.)

What's the best way to be heard above the general "noise?" I feel awkward, for instance, tweeting anything more than once, but know that all my followers may not be online at the exact same time. And Facebook keeps changing their algorithms, so I feel it's not reaching people as well as it used to.

First, never pay for ads on Facebook. Unless you are a corporation and sheer numbers are your game, don't do it. It actually negatively affects engagement, for complicated reasons.

Social media is the long game. You have to use it regularly, and use it well, and then, when you have something to promote, people will (a) accept your tweeting about your release for the morning and night crowd all week (assuming you tweet other things as well) and (b) listen. You have to be a good social media internet citizen and participate, and then you'll be rewarded. Social media is just human interaction. Be nice. Be interested in others. Promote good work that isn't yours. Give a little, get a little. Or get a lot, really.

What's your own strategy with your writing and social media?

I use my personal Twitter and Instagram all the time. I use Facebook less. I blog at least once a month (usually). I podcast. I've even started to play around with YouTube. Most of my tweets are dumb (hilarious) jokes and photos of my cats. When I come out with a new story or podcast project, I share them. I tag relevant parties on Twitter and Tumblr, and sometimes they read or listen, and that makes my day. I'm being followed by one of my favorite comics writers/artists on Twitter because he liked what I said about serial fiction.

Basically, my life goals are two-fold: 1. I want to make Good Art. 2. I want to make knowledge and art accessible—most ideally, free. I need to make a living, too, but if I can put it out there for free, I will. This is why I love social media. It's a culture of sharing. You make friends with people you've never met, and they become real friendships. You promote each other's work, and you purchase each other's work. I love Kickstarter, and I really love Patreon (and Gumroad)—there are all of these new methods of supporting one another financially and socially. My advice is to jump in! Participate. Learn. And don't be sad when you lose a follower, because they were either fishing for follows or aren't cool enough to appreciate your jokes.

CHAPTER 14: BALANCE YOUR PR AND CREATIVE EFFORTS

Avoid "Running To Stand Still" And Get Back Your Creative Juice

I don't know how many of you are old enough to remember one of U2's hits in *The Joshua Tree*, "Running to Stand Still?"

When it comes to marketing my books, I have frequently felt like I was "running to stand still." I especially felt this way when I was working as the Poet Laureate of Redmond, WA, while at the same time promoting a new book that had just come out. My own internal pressure as a Type-A personality made me feel that I should always be doing something to better myself, to make my book sell, to make myself a better writer, to build my local writing community. And I admit, I would sometimes hit a brick wall.

We writers put so much pressure on ourselves to be everything to everyone, and often this pressure has little impact on sales or anything worthwhile in the writing life. In the past, we could rely on publishers and their PR teams to do some of the salesmanship and PR for a book, but now, it's primarily up to us.

Aren't we supposed to be spending our valuable

time writing? I keep thinking, *Oh yes, I used to be a writer before I started worrying so much about all the other parts of being a writer besides writing!* Obviously, I don't consider blogging a couple of times a week a waste of time. It seems more like something worthwhile—reaching out to family and friends and a larger writing community and sharing.

Readings Are Worth It

Here is something else I don't consider a waste of time: readings. Sometimes they hurt—you drive a couple of hours, you don't get paid, a toddler screams through the entire reading, no one shows up, you go back home considering a life in a nice nunnery somewhere, or possibly some alternate universe space-pilot job. A lot of times readings can go awry, but not terribly—a fellow reader might not show up, but you meet people you might not have otherwise met, someone new connects with your work, or you're able to give someone support or encouragement at just the right time. Readings are still one of the best ways to connect your work to an audience, to meet your audience, to hear other writers and share ideas. You might experience a high school girl telling you she likes your way of looking at fairytales and she likes your earrings, or two people showing up who have never been to a poetry reading before and they're surprised at how much fun they had. There are some things that can happen at readings that can't happen anywhere else. So even if you are held back by realities, like having no money to tour, no time off from your job, fear of public speaking, or, like me, you struggle with staying healthy, you should remember that even with Facebook and blogs and Twitter, there are some things that have no substitute. Readings, from the sublime to the ridiculous, or the somewhere in-between, are invaluable for writers. And that's why you should do readings.

Give Yourself A Break

Writers, be kind to yourselves. Allow time to rest and recuperate and WRITE! If we stop running, I promise, the ground will not slip out from under us. A day or two off from the world (or Facebook or Twitter) is not going to be the end of your writing career. Determine how much time after a reading you need to recover. If you need more than a day, make sure not to stack events on top of each other or you may find yourself resenting what you've agreed to do. Recovery might take longer than a day or two if you have health or other personal challenges in your life.

Remember the good things: the moment you write something new that you are pleased with, the smile on the face of someone at a reading when they're listening to your work, when you find an editor or publisher who really *gets* your work. Those are the reasons we keep at this crazy life.

CHAPTER 15: PURSUE THE ELUSIVE REVIEW

Tips For Getting Your Book Reviewed

I have been reviewing books, independently, for over a decade now. Occasionally, though not often, I get paid for it. In this chapter, I'll provide tips, based on my personal experience, on what the best strategies are for getting your books reviewed. Before we start, you need the inside scoop on how the review process works.

How Book Reviews Are Assigned

Some book reviews are assigned, and in this case, the reviewer doesn't receive any input in what he/she reviews. This is how it typically works for reviews that the reviewer gets paid to write. Sometimes, journals have certain reviewers that they like. These reviewers are offered a list of books by the journal and the reviewers have their choice. And, sometimes, reviewers will pitch a review idea to a journal, magazine, or blog.

Personally, I try not to review books by close friends, students, or mentors in any journals or magazines, but only on my blog, Amazon, or Goodreads. I want to avoid the appearance of a conflict of interest. Journals tend to prefer that you not review close acquaintances, but the rules can bend occasionally.

An active reviewer usually receives 50-100 books a year sent by publishers or authors for review. That's on top of what they buy themselves or are assigned. You can do the math: most books sent to reviewers do not get reviewed.

Getting a review published, even when the reviewer really likes the book, is much harder now than it was five years ago. I know this from personal experience. There are fewer outlets publishing reviews and paying for reviews, and those that do aren't giving as much space to reviews as they used to. So the reality is, you will need to work hard as a writer to get your book reviewed. If you have a publisher that is sending out review copies for you, that's fantastic! Some will provide an unlimited number of advance review copies (known fondly as ARCs). However, in many cases, extra review copies come out of your pocket. Hence, I am providing tips for you to be as efficient with your review copies as possible.

Target Your Review Copies

Maybe you'll end up reviewed in *The New York Times Review of Books* or *The Atlantic*. It's possible. But you'll probably get more return on your investment if you target either literary journals that have liked your work in the past or reviewers whose work might be similar to yours. For instance, if you're writing feminist superhero poetry, I'm probably a great reviewer for you to target. But how would you know that unless you read some of my work? Sometimes reading the actual poetry of the person doing the reviews is a great way to get insight into the reviewer's aesthetic. Also, look up reviewers who have reviewed books you like, or books that are similar to yours, and contact them to see if they would be interested in reviewing your book.

Write A Personal Note

I get tons of review copies with no note. I usually can't remember whether I requested a particular book because the time between the request and receiving the copy could be months. So, remember to put a slip of paper in your book that reads: *Hi there! Remember when you said you'd be interested in my series of triolets on the Old West at the Old West Poetry Conference? Well, now it's out, and I'd sure appreciate your take on the book!* Or something like that. By the way, this was the number one tip that reviewers posted when I asked this question on Facebook. You'd be surprised how few people (or publishers) put in a personal note.

Follow Up

Don't be embarrassed to follow up with people who have promised to write reviews for you. Many times, as a reviewer, I've just forgotten or misplaced the books I was planning to consider for reviews. I think if more people followed up with an email after sending me their books, I would probably be more likely to give their book a serious read.

Give Your Reviewers A List Of Publication Options

As an active reviewer of poetry books, I feel I need to reiterate this point. It can be hard to get poetry book reviews published, even thoughtful and well-written ones. So, if you know of an outlet (journal, magazine, or blog) that might be receptive to publishing a review of your book, let your reviewers know about it. This is a key step that few people take. Don't put all of the work in the lap of the reviewer. Did I mention that reviewers are usually writing reviews in their spare time for no pay? So, anything you can do to assist in placing your review is much appreciated. Do a little reconnaissance— write to a few editors to see if they might be open to a review. Then, mention those editors and the names of their journals to your targeted reviewer. Voilà! Literary matchmaking!

Make It As Easy As Possible

Include a press kit when you send your book to a reviewer. Write a short summary of your book in your personal note. Reviewer Julie Brooks Barbour posted on my Facebook query on this topic: *I review books based on the narrative structure, of what threads the book together. If the narrative is unclear to me, I probably won't review it.* This again comes down to targeting your reviewers and doing more than only sending a copy of your book without a note or further information.

After Your Follow Up

Here is some important advice: Don't expect anything, don't hold grudges, and contact the reviewer again when your next book comes out because . . . things happen. As a reviewer, I might love someone's first book, but not connect with someone's second book. I might be unable to successfully pitch a review of your book to anyone. I might get overloaded and burned out and take a short break from reviewing. I would say the success rate from a good, targeted book mailing might be 20 percent. If you hold a grudge against a reviewer for not reviewing one of your books, or a journal for not running a review, that means you've lost a potential review or review venue for your next venture, and that would be a shame. Because you're writing more than one book, right? You're in for the long haul.

Write A Few Reviews Yourself!

Before asking others to review your book, try to write a book review yourself and get it published in a literary journal, magazine, or blog. This will give you a better perspective on how reviews work from the inside out. I confess that I tend to Google everyone I review because I like to do a little research on the people I'm writing about. If I see that an author has been reviewing books, I'm more likely to review his/her book because I've seen that he/she is an active reviewer. If I'm putting a lot of volunteer labor into reviewing, and I'm a writer myself who could be writing poems or doing paid work, then I probably want to review authors who are also doing some work by putting positive energy back into the literary universe.

Bless all the editors working for free in their spare time and the reviewers who pour their souls into trying to create some kind of intelligent discourse about books and the publishers who put their own income into marketing the books they produce. This comes down to karma, karma, karma.

Should I Pay For Reviews?

As an author, you will probably hear that if you spend some money you can guarantee book reviews. There are two services in particular that can be useful for you to generate reviews of your book, NetGalley and *Kirkus Reviews*. Both services can get pricey (they are mostly used by large publishers with deep pockets), but I would like to mention them for the sake of being thorough.

There are also "book blog tours" where you get reviewed on multiple book blogs. Most of these services are for pay, though you don't have to coordinate them—that's the service you're paying for. I discuss these services more in *Chapter 23: Book Promotion Services*.

Tips From An Expert

Victoria Chang, who's on the teaching faculty at Antioch's MFA program, has had her book *Barbie Chang* reviewed in outlets like *Publisher's Weekly, Library Journal*, and *The San Francisco Chronicle*. She has this advice for new poets sending out their books in hopes of receiving reviews:

Copper Canyon sent out the book, so their PR people did their thing. I gave my publisher all my own ideas and the people I know. They combined my list with their own . . . there wasn't any magic in this process. I've been writing poetry in this community for some time. I think that for new writers with first books you may not get that many reviews, and I think that's OK. You might not get any review, and I think that's OK. Maybe for future books you will. Just focus on the work. The work will bring in reviews.

Outlets That Publish Poetry Reviews

Here is a (non-exhaustive) list of my favorite outlets

that are publishing reviews of poetry books (at the time of this publication):

- *Tupelo Quarterly*
- *Rain Taxi*
- *The Rumpus*
- *Mid-American Review*
- *Pleiades*
- *Strange Horizons* (for speculative books of poetry)
- *Star*Line* (for speculative books of poetry)
- *The Library Journal*
- *The American Book Review*
- *American Poetry Review*
- *The New York Times Review of Books*
- *Women's Review of Books*

Action Items:

1. If you haven't ever done this before, consider writing a book review. Start small: an Amazon or Goodreads review for a poetry book you feel really enthusiastic about.

2. Begin a strategy for querying literary magazines

or review outlets to write reviews of contemporary poetry books.

3. Put together a list of potential reviewers and include both snail mail and e-mail contact information for sending e-galleys and print galleys. Write to them to see if they're interested. Go!

CHAPTER 16: SELLING MORE BOOKS

A Practical Guide To Improving Your Numbers

We've discussed where to sell your book. So, the obvious question is, *What can the average poet with a book coming out do to make sure he/she sells a decent number of copies?* People (and publishers) have different ideas of how many sales make a poetry book successful. Some poetry books, even contest-winning books, will only sell 100-200 copies. But, don't despair. I'm here to say it's possible to sell 1,000 copies of your poetry book (or even 10,000—it happens!).

Generating sales is easier for well-known poets (Danez Smith, Claudia Rankine, Rupi Kauer, Billy Collins, Mary Oliver) with large national publishers. But for "regular" poets who aren't superstars and whose books are published by small indie presses (without dedicated PR folks or a big budget), how can you make it work? There's no single magic recipe, but let's take a look at some things you can do.

Think Big!

Getting the word out about your book is tough if you're a poet with a small press, but not impossible. If you receive a starred review in *Publisher's Weekly*, or a review in *Shelf Awareness*, or you are picked up by The Rumpus Book Club, or your book is mentioned in *Oprah* or *Elle* or another major magazine—these lucky breaks can make a big difference to your book. You can't make this kind of publicity happen, but it *could* happen. Make sure you and your publisher work together to target a few of the major media outlets, even if they are long shots.

Can You Hear Me Now?

Here is something weird—even with all of my social media activity (including my blog, Facebook, Twitter), my friends and some close family members will still say: "You have a book coming out?" I feel like I've been announcing my new book over and over, but people may or may not be paying attention. Remember, there's a lot of noise on the internet and what you consider a "shout" may be a whisper. You don't want to oversaturate your audience of friends and family with notices, but on the other hand, a postcard, an email announcement, and posting on Facebook and Twitter is NOT overkill. Because chances are, most people will overlook three of those four notices. And those are the people that already like you.

Expand Your Sales Options

You can sell more books by increasing and diversifying the opportunities to sell your book. Consider doing some of the following:

- **Set up readings.** Promoting your book at readings can work well especially if you're a good performer. However, it's not everyone's bag. You will learn more in *Chapter 20: Your Book Tour.*

- **Get your book taught.** If you can convince teachers to add your book to their college or high school curriculum, you will potentially have a steady flow of sales for years. Success often depends heavily on subject matter and who you know. You will learn more in *Chapter 30: Win in the Classroom.*

- **Book clubs**. Oprah's Book Club has made many authors famous and created bestsellers. Getting your book into local book clubs can be a win. You will learn more in *Chapter 31: Go Clubbing.*

- **Get people to talk about your book**. PR in the form of reviews, interviews, blog book tours, local radio, social media, and simple word of mouth can drive sales. It helps if you're a superstar, but most of us aren't superstars; having a great personality is a plus—graciousness and kindness go a long way. You will learn more about radio in *Chapter 17:*

Rocking on the Radio.

- **Attend a conference.** If you are regular attendee or presenter at a professional conference or ComicCon, this might be a good place to sell your book. There is usually a conference bookstore that will sell your book for you if you are a presenter. Try to show up at AWP (if you can afford it—for those unaffiliated with a university, the trip usually runs about $1500 with flight and accommodations). If the AWP Conference is happening in your town, you must go. You may not get your book on a sales table, but you will likely run into people who are interested (and it's a great place to scope out and meet publishers).

Stay Realistic

I think the most important aspect about sales is to not expect the book to sell itself. Also, don't expect the publisher to do all the work. If you go into your book promotion with realistic expectations, knowing you will need to put in a certain amount of time and effort, you can avoid going from the "I'm going to publish a book" ecstasy to the depths of "I've published a book, but no one cares" depression.

Action Items:

1. Consider a small achievable goal, like: I will sell five books this week through promotions on social media.

2. Check and confirm that you are doing everything you can to help your publisher get the word out about your book. Once again, the goal is not to annoy people, but to let interested audiences know that your book is out there.

3. Spend some time in local bookstores, and talk to the person in charge of purchases. You can suggest that they carry your book and offer something in return—such as promoting their bookstore on social media.

CHAPTER 17: ROCKING ON THE RADIO

"Old Media" Still Works

Local and national radio stations—particularly NPR and its affiliates—can promote books, and one radio spot can equal lots of sales. When I was a brand-new author, my publisher sent my first book to *The Writer's Almanac*—and two different poems were read from the book. This resulted in sales—I could watch the Amazon rank get better and better as the day went on. I've also had a local reading posted on our local NPR affiliate's website, as well as an interview and a poem written for the Fukushima anniversary. And when one of my poems was on the radio, I was in our local poetry-only bookstore, and a person came in off the street asking for the book *by Jeannine something . . . she was just on the radio . . . something with villainess?* Ha!

Often your publisher can help you get this kind of major publicity, but sometimes you might have contacts who work at a local radio or television station. If that's the case, offer them (nicely, with no pressure) a copy of your book to take a look at. You never know what might come of it! Remember, just because radio is "old media," it doesn't mean it can't sell books. It's valuable spending some time researching your local "old media" outlets.

Interview With Elizabeth Austen

For more advice on radio and poetry, I interviewed Elizabeth Austen, former Poet Laureate of Washington State. Austen is not only a fine writer, but she is a literary producer for Seattle's local NPR network affiliate, KUOW. She also gives coaching sessions for reading on the radio for writers in the Jack Straw Program, which benefits WA State artists. She talks about her new book and gives tips on how poets can be better on the radio.

Elizabeth, you're a professional interviewer for our local Seattle NPR station, KUOW. What advice do you have for poets preparing for a radio interview?

Though I'm called a "literary producer," I have the luxury of focusing exclusively on poetry for KUOW. I produce a weekly poetry segment, introducing a Pacific NW poet and his or her poem. I also do occasional interviews, and have had the pleasure of talking with poets including W.S. Merwin, Jane Hirshfield, Mark Doty, Eavan Boland and Chris Abani.

When preparing for a radio interview, I recommend listening to an example or two of your interviewer's program, so that you'll have a sense of what to expect in terms of tone and approach. Does this interviewer tend to ask more about craft and process, or about the backstory of the book or individual poems? Is the interviewer looking for anecdotes and stories? Does it seem like the interviewer has actually read the book?

I recommend that you spend some time thinking about what YOU want to say about your work. Very often, the person interviewing you will not have had time to read your book, and may or may not feel confident discussing poetry. What do you want to tell listeners about how you developed the collection, your personal connection to the subject matter, why and how you write, etc? Which poems will be a good introduction to the book, especially for someone who may not usually (or ever) read poetry? You're essentially interviewer-proofing yourself. Hopefully you'll get an interviewer who is genuinely interested in you and your book, but you can't depend on that.

I'm a great believer in preparing for anything, and then letting go of the preparation during the interview so you can respond to what's actually happening in the conversation. The preparation will be there for you—you can trust that and relax and enjoy talking about your work.

Any tips for reading poems on the air? Any differences you would want poets to note between our usual "live" readings and one for radio or recording?

Yes—keep it short. I was interviewed by Radio New Zealand in 2006, and despite my experience doing radio myself, I made the mistake of bringing long (more than one page) poems to the interview. The result was that they had to excerpt them—not ideal! Make sure the poems you read are reasonably accessible, too—remember that radio listeners are almost surely multi-tasking.

Think about how you'll introduce the poem—you might want to give a little more information than you would at a reading, where you (hopefully!) have your listeners' undivided attention.

How are you using audio to promote your book, Every Dress a Decision*?*

I had the good fortune to be interviewed by Steve Scher on KUOW's Weekday just as the book was launching (along with Billy Collins, which was fun and kind of surreal), so I have a link to that on my blog and I shared it on Facebook. Now that I'm through the first, intense round of readings, I can start thinking about ways to use audio to promote the book—check back with me in six months!

How would you recommend that a poet approach his/her local radio station for a feature?

Start with your local NPR-affiliate and community radio stations. The most important thing to do is to scour the station's website to find out which (if any, let's be frank) programs and producers cover poetry. Then listen to some examples of their poetry-related programming. (If you don't do this homework first, you're likely wasting your time and review copies.) Start with an e-mail, introducing yourself as a local writer and describing your book. Include the press release and local reading dates, and inquire if you can send a review copy.

If you're touring with your book, check the sites of the NPR affiliates in the cities where you're reading. If they feature poetry, send an e-mail with the dates that you're in town and where you'll be reading, your book's press release, and an offer to send a review copy. If you've got any audio of yourself being interviewed or reading online, include a link.

The important thing is to remember that producers are looking for content that fits their programming needs. If you do a little work up front, you can write your e-mail in such a way that you show how you are a good fit with their program. Make it easy for them by keeping your correspondence brief and professional—you know, the same way you'd approach the editor of a journal.

I've featured lots of poets on KUOW who approached me first via e-mail, whose work I didn't yet know. Now it's time for me to take my own advice and write some queries! Good luck putting your work out there—radio is a terrific medium for connecting with new readers!

CHAPTER 18: LEVERAGE LIBRARIES

Encourage Libraries To Stock Your Book

One of the best ways to sell several books at once is to get your book on librarians' purchasing list. Not only do libraries purchase book copies, but they make them available to readers who might not otherwise get exposed to your work.

Make Friends With Librarians

Clearly, you can't befriend all librarians, but you can acquaint yourself with many. A great way to start is to visit your own local library on a regular basis and talk to the librarians there. Give them a copy of your PR kit before your book comes out. Look at their poetry catalogue and see how your book might fit in. For instance, tell them that you're a local author and the subject matter of your book might be connected to other reading promotions that they're running.

Get Reviewed In Library Trade Journals

Librarians pay attention to a few specific journals, which are related to book publishing: *Publisher's Weekly* (a long shot for most of us with small presses, but still a possibility), *Booklist*, *Kirkus Review*, *Midwest Book Review*, and *The Library Journal*. This is one reason you want to have your publisher prepare an e-galley and a PR kit six months in advance of your book coming out—it's a requirement in order to receive mention in some of these journals.

Win Awards

Okay, I know this one's not fair—but librarians pay attention to who wins the significant book awards. Win one of these, and you will get major uptake into library systems around the world (and lots of other things will improve as well). I discuss more about published book prizes in *Chapter 28: Eye On The Prize*.

Have Friends Request Your Book

Most libraries accept requests from their patrons about which books to purchase—essentially how to spend their procurement budgets. Whenever I move to a new area, one of the first things I do is to open a library account. Most libraries let you place a book request online, but it's probably not as effective for authors to request their own books. In addition, some libraries require that a book be requested 2-5 times before they will order a copy. This is a tough one, and I have a hard time asking anyone but my best friends and my parents to do it. But we should be asking people to request our books at their local libraries—especially those who write to tell us how much they love our work. If you talk to students, for example, remind them that they can request your book at their college library.

Tips From Librarians

Here are some insights from several librarians about how they decide on which books to purchase for their collections.

From Anne Haines, who works at the Indiana University libraries:

In our huge academic library, a lot of our books are selected via approval plan—basically we set up a profile with a vendor and receive all of the books that fit that profile. For example, from a particular university press that our distributor carries, we might get all of their poetry, film studies, nineteenth and twentieth century history except for Slavic and East Asian, and none of their other subject areas. (That is a totally made up and likely less than realistic profile, but you get the idea.) Beyond that, we'd probably pick up major award winners and titles recommended by faculty or students, and if the bibliographer has time, she might check reviews in journals such as Choice or Library Journal. We are so huge, and our bibliographers have so many other duties, that title by title hand selection just isn't really going to happen. Faculty recommendations do count for a lot. Contacting the library directly is ok but try to get your materials sent to the right person—not just to the reference desk or the administrative office. Since I don't manage any subjects I can't tell you how many unsolicited flyers, e-mails, etc. they get or how many of those actually have any effect. We get a lot of self-published authors trying to peddle books of little interest to an academic audience (family history, badly written fiction, etc.)—I know that because a lot of their e-mails and phone calls come in to the reference desk. Some libraries (ours included, though I'm certain we're not the only one) offer a "suggest a purchase" form on their website, and using this form would at least ensure that the solicitation goes to the right person.

From Jeremy Brett, the Curator of the Fantasy and Science Fiction Library at Texas A&M University:

As the one who buys the Sci-Fi poetry for the Libraries, I can say that I often go for the books that win or are nominated for awards. I also try to look for what I think are unique voices, or works written by underrepresented groups. Also, since we're a Texas institution, I also look for poets from TX or the Borderlands.

So, the takeaway seems to be: win awards, try to interest your local area libraries in your book, and use the "suggest a purchase" form—or send a link to it for friends to use.

Find Your Book In Libraries

If you want to see if your book is already in libraries or how effective your PR with librarians has been, there's a great site for this information—Worldcat.org lets you search for your book by ISBN number, and it shows you the libraries that have it in their catalog, starting with the library closest to you. My small press books are usually in 30-50 libraries. Books published in a major university press series will often be found in hundreds of libraries.

Action Items:

1. Talk to your local librarian in charge of purchases. Be friendly, polite, and bring in a PR packet to give to them. You can offer to do a reading at the library as an incentive.

2. Use WorldCat to track which libraries are carrying your books. It's always exciting to see your book showing up in new towns and at new universities.

3. Ask your friends and family to order a copy of your new book from their local libraries. This is free and a great way to get the word out.

CHAPTER 19: THE LAUNCH PARTY

Get The Most Out Of The Big Day

Your book launch is a little bit like a wedding—it can be as big or as intimate as you like, it can take months of planning, and it involves getting up in front of your friends and family. Whatever you decide, make the book launch a party. People love to celebrate your success with you.

No One Hates A Party

So many people aren't excited about poetry readings, but no one hates a party! So if your venue allows it, bring in champagne and snacks to celebrate after the reading. If the venue does not allow food or drinks, maybe plan to meet afterwards at a local bar or restaurant. One year, I planned my book launch to coincide with my 40th birthday party—it was probably my most successful book launch and most successful birthday party. It helps, of course, to have a significant other—be it a helpful spouse or best friend—who can pitch in and organize the party part, because you might be zonked to the point of speaking in single syllables by the time you get there. If you have reserved a separate venue for the after party, ask a significant other or good friend to arrive early to make sure all is arranged before your guests arrive.

Think Outside The Bookstore

When it comes to a venue, everyone wants to launch their book in a bookstore. While these businesses attract book lovers, they may not always be configured for large gatherings or allow food and drinks. Other potential launch party venues are local parks (with covered areas), restaurants, art centers, and even wineries.

I've seen book launch parties and readings at people's houses, and I have had a successful launch party at my house. This is a great idea when you have a good entertaining space that is close to many of your friends or when your budget is limited. Granted, you may not want to host a public reading at your home, but my home launch party was a success when I just invited my friends.

Host Multiple Parties

Why not have more than one launch party? For my first book, I paired up with another poet from the same press, and we had a reading and book party here in Seattle. Then, I went to my hometown of Cincinnati, where my parents threw another book party, which included a short reading and book signing. Finally, I traveled to my publisher's hometown for a reading, where he and his family threw another party afterwards. At this party, there were cookies decorated with art from the book cover. If you can afford the travel, and you're booking readings, having a party is the best way to meet people, have good conversations with local writers and friends, and enjoy a little down time and cake. I have also seen authors call each book reading in a different city a "launch." "Launch Reading for Portland," and "Launch Reading for Santa Clara" as each location is really the first reading for your book, geographically speaking. Bottom line: "Readings" seem boring. "Parties" seem fun.

Include Others

You may be deceived into thinking your book launch is all about you, but you will have a lot less stress and more fun if you include at least one poet or artist friend in the event. I only did one book launch reading by myself, by request of the venue, and let me tell you, it was the most stressful and the least fun for me. For *Field Guide to the End of the World*, I had a friend and poet serve as emcee and opening reader, which worked great. I was off the hook for at least fifteen minutes of the reading, the crowd loved them, I loved them, and it made the whole event a lot more fun, and less focused on only me. Also, having an emcee and/or opening reader, brings new people from their networks and communities to the reading.

If you can, as I did with *Becoming the Villainess*,

hook up with another author from the same press who has a book coming out around the same time. This way, you get more bang for your buck and you reach each other's audience. If you have no poetry friends in the area, ask a local poet, who you might know through Facebook or Twitter, to read with you.

Plan Far In Advance

You might need to book well-known venues (both reading and party) a full six months ahead of the planned event. This is especially true when you want a popular spot, like a literary center or famous bookstore or hot restaurant. Because we often don't have that lead time from publishers, especially small publishers, plan the event on a date after your publisher tells you the book will be out. (*Field Guide to the End of the World* came out September 1st, and my reading event at a local winery was in mid-September.) This gives you a little leeway if, as things often happen, the publisher can't get you the books by the release date, or the bookstore you're reading at doesn't have the books from the distributor by the release date.

Often venues will charge money for your event, but sometimes they won't. For my launch of *The Robot Scientist's Daughter*, the kind people at the local Jack Straw Cultural Center not only gave me the space for free, but they also wrote a grant to fund the book launch. Talk about supporting local writers! But, especially in larger cities or if you're involving restaurants and theatre spaces, realize there will likely be some money involved. You will want to consider your PR budget carefully. Your book launch will likely be a PR cost, unless you are able to line up a free venue or arrange for a donated space. Think about any organizations in your area that support the arts. If there is a gallery you frequent or your community has a local community center, consider inquiring if they would be open to a poetry reading. Many community centers don't change for events— you only need to make a reservation.

Send Out Invitations

Send out paper and email and Facebook event invitations. Multiple invitations always increase the number of people who will remember your event. Even your good friends can hear about your book launch a handful of times before they will remember and put it into their calendars. Create a public event on Facebook and invite your friends, but also send paper invitations to the group of people you most want there, and send Evites (an email invitation service at evite.com) to all friends and acquaintances.

You really cannot over-invite. I can be shy about this one; I invited about thirty to forty people to my latest book launch, and one of my friends told me, "You haven't invited enough people." If you want forty to show up, invite eighty. This is especially true during the summer and the holiday season.

Send information about your event to local newspapers. One of my book launches was listed in the local alternative weekly as a "local pick" for the weekend, and lots of new faces turned up at that reading. Check out your local newspaper's events page, as there are often guidelines on how to let them know about your event.

Be Mindful Of Timing

On the day of one of my launch events for *She Returns to the Floating World,* President Obama visited Seattle, and the security detail shut down all of the highways that gave access to my venue from every direction. It took me an hour and a half to arrive at the venue, which is typically twenty minutes away. Very few people showed up on time. Now, there was no way to know about this beforehand because President Obama had not announced his arrival, but plan your event on a night that's not featuring a major sporting event (no going up against the Super Bowl) or some other event that jams up highways and pulls away your potential guests. The exception to this? If your town is having a weeklong literary event or hosting the AWP

Conference, having your launch at this time is probably a great idea, because you'll be able to attract the literary crowds that are in your area.

Be Ready To Sell

As fun as a party is, part of the reason you have gone to the trouble of planning it is to sell your book. If you can, have a point-of-sale app on your device (smartphone or tablet) that will accept credit cards. PayPal and Stripe are two apps that are popular. For the apps to work properly, be sure that the venue has Wi-Fi or a cell signal. Also, bring $30 to $40 in small bills (especially $1 and $5 bills) for making change—someone always shows up with a $50 or $100 bill.

As the host of your launch party, you may be too busy to sell books yourself. Ask a friend or family member to assist you in selling books as you'll be signing your books and socializing. It's a relief not to worry about money-changing while you're in the midst of your party. If you are fortunate enough to have your reading in a bookstore, they will probably provide the bookselling personnel, but they will take a consignment cut of your sales if you have brought your own books to the store with a consignment agreement.

Offer A Takeaway

Bring some of your swag to give people as a thank you for coming to the reading and party. For festive treats think champagne, sparkling cider, cake, petit fours, or any other treats that will be a hit at your gathering. Take time to actually celebrate. We poets don't get enough chances to do that!

Action Items:

1. Make a list of places that would be good venues for a book launch. Think outside the box.

2. In thinking about your launch, consider dates, times, cost, location, etc. Make a budget for how much you can afford to spend, and look at your calendar for dates when you will be free. Also be sure the date does not coincide with an event that will make your reading difficult for people to attend.

3. Create some sample swag for your book. Start small, maybe with your business card or a bookmark. If you have already created swag, decide which items would be best to give away at your launch.

4. Ask your friends and family if they would like

to participate, and if so, how? Would they like to emcee? Help sell books or bring friends to the reading? Not everyone will want to participate, but for the ones who do—give them treats like cupcakes or pizza, and offer to reciprocate at their book launches. And remember to send thank you notes to the venue and to all who took an active part in your event.

CHAPTER 20: YOUR BOOK TOUR

Promoting Your Book Both Online And In Real Life

Book tours can be virtual, like a blog book tour, or in real life (IRL), such as traveling to bookstores, libraries, literary centers, or college campuses. At these venues you can read from your book and/or teach workshops as well as interact with local writers.

At the beginning of my poetry career, a non-poet friend of mine, who was a former VP of marketing at a Fortune 500 company, asked, "So, what do poets do to, you know, get the word out about their work?" I answered timidly, "Well, we wait until a college asks us to visit and read, and sometimes we read for free at coffee shops and independent bookstores." Needless to say, she was not impressed with this plan—it's not practical if you want to reach people who might not be familiar with poetry.

So what should we be doing? Why aren't more poets (and poetry publishers) more ambitious about getting poetry out to more people who aren't already poets or poetry lovers? Consider not only some time-honored practices for book tours, but also some less conventional ideas, like selling your book at art exhibits and visiting WonderCon.

Touring IRL

Touring "in real life" is the old-school way of doing a book tour—the way most of us are familiar with. An author travels—most of the time on his/her own dime, but sometimes on the dime of publishers, universities, literary centers, and other groups—to a bookstore, a library, a book club meeting, or maybe an art gallery, festival, or conference.

It's every poet's goal to be paid to host workshops, teach a class, and do readings at universities and writing centers across the country. There are also literary festivals and conferences, usually in the summer, which sometimes pay an author to read and attend the events. These festivals and conferences can be useful in making new connections as well as selling books to new readers in a different locale. In the Northwest, two of our biggest conferences and festivals focusing on poetry are the Skagit River Poetry Festival and the Port Townsend Writer's Conference. On the East Coast, the Dodge Festival and the Massachusetts Poetry Festival are well-known literary gatherings. An example of a more loosely-organized literary event is LitQuake in San Francisco, where a ton of readings happen all around the area during a couple of days in the fall. These loosely-organized events may not pay, but are often worth reading at because of the connections, the crowds, and the fun!

In your own area and in surrounding areas, look for established reading series that already have good attendance, as this increases your chance of having an audience and making new connections. These series are held everywhere from arts centers and schools to cafes and bookstores. If you have spent time attending your city's readings, it can make a difference, especially if you have become acquainted with the person running the series. You can ask about setting up a reading and you might have a better chance than someone who has never attending a reading there before.

The last—and hardest—type of reading to set up on your tour is cold calling (or cold emailing) a bookstore, library, or education center to ask for a reading. I suggest that you write or call the contact person of these events and explain who you are, what your book is about, and ideally, a time that you are available to read. Do this a few months in advance of your desired date. Your readings can be for you alone, but I will tell you from experience, it's much better when your readings include other people, especially locals, if you're outside of your home area. Having a good sell sheet at this point is helpful for handing to (or emailing) bookstore or literary center representatives.

Sandra Beasley's tips from Chapter 8 also apply here and are worth repeating:

- Friendly opening relating your connection to the store (ideally, you have been there at least once) or the area.

- Brief description of your book: genre, theme, press, publication date. If it won a prize in tandem with your publication, mention that.

- Platform for crowd draw. Do you have a nearby academic affiliation? Are you open to pairing with a local reader?

- Range of dates available for reading. Be sure to specify if you're available for weekends, weeknights, or both.

- Small JPG of your cover art; let them know both cover art and author photo are available in high resolution if needed.

- Be sure to close with your full contact information.

This is something I have done—thinking outside the box when it comes to venues. I've sold as many books at "cons"—places like GeekGirlCon, WonderCon, and ComicCon—as I have at traditional book conferences or writers' groups. If your book's theme is genealogy or medicine, find your audience and offer to speak at genealogy group meetings or medical conferences.

Online Book Tours And Blog Book Tours

A huge online universe of book lovers, book reviewers, book websites, and book blogs has developed over the last few years. There are book blog sites that focus on cookbooks, cozy mysteries, children's books, and even, yes, poetry! But don't limit yourself to poetry-related book sites—if your book has an environmental angle, reach out to environmental book reviewers or websites.

The easiest way to do an "online book tour" is to ask some of your favorite book blogs if they would be interested in "hosting" you on your blog book tour. Perhaps they will post a review your book, interview you, or ask you to write a guest post where you casually work in that you have a new book out. Definitely ask your friends who blog if they would be interested in helping you out in this way. Large publishers can arrange "blog book tours" for their authors, which often go beyond American "blog book tours," to include Canadian, British, Australian, and Irish blogs—places that reach English-speaking readers.

Action Items:

1. Brainstorm places to visit where you can reach new people. Include your current town, but also think of your hometown, maybe your

alma mater's town, and places where you have friends and family willing to put you up for a night and come out to see you!

2. Contact a few bookstores and literary centers within a two-hour radius of your home. Offer ideas—a reading paired with a Q&A session; a workshop on generating new work or nature writing or ekphrastic poetry.

CHAPTER 21: DON'T PANIC!

A Few Words For First-Time Poetry Book Authors

I have an ambitious, smart, hardworking writer friend who just launched her first poetry book. She is very anxious for it to do well. I remember feeling anxiety when my first book came out. Type A personalities especially have this problem. Anxiety doesn't always serve you well in the nerve-wracking ride of first book launches.

Any Reading Where You Sell Books Is a Good Reading

In the course of publishing five books of poetry, I've done hundreds of readings. Some great, some not as great. Over the years, I've learned to be thankful if:

1) No one falls asleep or walks out
2) More than six people show up
3) I sell any books at all

For many poets, readings take a lot of emotional and physical energy, and some readings don't "pay off." You learn as you go that there are good days for reading and bad ones, and most times, you don't have control over how they turn out. For instance, bars are typically louder than a bookstore and more likely to have rowdy locals not as interested in poetry. (Although I once did a reading at a wine bar where a completely sauced woman bought everyone's books and gave us hugs!) Bookstores are more likely to be quiet, but are also more likely to be empty, especially if they haven't promoted your reading well.

Like *The Hitchhiker's Guide To The Galaxy* Told You— Don't Panic

Most books of poetry do not sell 1,000 copies, so try not to feel bad if you're not selling out of the one hundred books you bought from your publisher. It takes time for poetry books to gather steam from word of mouth, positive reviews, good readings, and all the other promotion you've done for your book. "Buzz" matters, but for poetry books, it's more of a slow-but-steady buzz that helps you in the long run. Rarely do poets become rich from their poetry book royalties. Even Billy Collins occasionally does readings in exchange for time on a golf course and free wine. I have it on good authority!

Making You Book Stand Out Is Difficult

This isn't meant to discourage people, but there is an abundance of poetry books published every year. Check out the poetry-only bookstore, Open Books in Seattle, or visit the website Poetry Daily (www.poems.com) to get the sense of how many books are out there. While it may seem like a tough challenge to make noise when everyone is shouting, the best advice I have is to find your target audience and connect with those readers. If you've written a book with poems about airline pilots, it may be useful to find airline pilot websites and events. If your book has a regional slant, maybe contact local newspapers or the NPR affiliate. Determine what makes your book unique from other poetry books and research media outlets and communities (Facebook groups, newsletters, podcasts, blogs, book groups, etc.) that may be open to featuring your book.

As a new author, no one knows about you yet, so it's your job to educate new readers as to who you are. I advise poets to create a clean basic author website, have a presence on Facebook, Twitter, Instagram, or Tumblr, and perhaps, start a blog. Remember, with each action to connect, you are building a presence in the real world and in the virtual world. You are finding your audience (and they are finding you) so working to make your book stand out may require some patience. The readers will come, eventually. Building an audience is a long game, not a short one.

Do What You're Best At

Some people are terrific at giving readings and workshops and interacting with new people, while others are not. Some individuals are good at interacting on Twitter, and while I'm not one of them, I'm still on Twitter. Find what you're best at, and shine there. Maybe for you this means speaking to Chamber of Commerce groups or at senior centers or high schools. Maybe you shine at writing kickass articles on your book's topic and getting them published. Or maybe you're more visual, so you create and post videos about your book. Find and exploit your own talents.

Don't Take It Personally

Your friends and family might forget about your book, even if you have sent them an email and a postcard announcing your publication. You and your book aren't the center of other people's universes. People might forget to attend your readings or they will write bad reviews of your book on Amazon. (Yup, my first book has my only one-star Amazon review— and whatcha gonna do?) I remember a friend who was angry when her book got four stars instead of five on Goodreads. That's going to happen, especially as your book gets picked up by non-friends and family. To many readers, a four-star review is considered a good enough recommendation. You have to let it go. You can't let it personally disappoint you, or you're going to get bitter. You need that energy to write your next book!

You're Going To Write Again So Get On With It

Your first book will probably not be your one and only, right? So even in the middle of your book tours and promotional work, remember to keep writing and submitting your work to literary journals and magazines. Keeping your writing life engaged will also help give you more energy to deal with bad reviews or readings where three people attend. You can think, "Sure, this is hard, but wait until my next book!" So much about the writing life is your attitude and your energy. Remember, promoting the book is just part of the journey, and it's something that you do while also thinking about the great work you're going to produce next.

CHAPTER 22: BOOK PROMOTION SERVICES

Spending Money To (Hopefully) Get Some Reviews

There are many book promotion services you can sign up for with varying results and for varying amounts of money. The services that I cover in this chapter offer you the opportunity to get your book reviewed, although your mileage may vary. Most of these services will not be targeted to poetry audiences, and since poetry books are not usually huge money makers, the cost can be prohibitive.

Book Blog Tours

With my last two books, I signed up for the Poetic Book Tours services because it is run by Serena Agusto-Cox, a reviewer I trust. This particular service, which starts at a few hundred dollars, arranges for a series of coordinated reviews of your book on a variety of smaller but reputable blogs. In the following chapter, I have an interview with Serena, and it includes her suggestions for book blog touring. She doesn't guarantee positive reviews, but she does coordinate and manage the process of getting your book galley (or e-galley) out to people she trusts and who already have an audience. The number of reviews is determined by how many of the book blog managers are interested in your book and how many like it enough to spend the time reviewing it. I felt lucky in the number of reviews I received, even on book blogs that were not necessarily poetry-focused.

Review Services

Kirkus Reviews has an "indie books" service—costly—that will get your book reviewed. It does NOT promise a positive review, and no one will know that your review was a paid review. I find the whole process a little ethically dicey, although maybe not?

NetGalley is an interesting tool that allows publishers and authors (for a fee—usually around $400 a book) to post an e-galley of their book, which is distributed to a wide range of readers—librarians, bookstore owners, independent reviewers, and people who sign up to receive e-galleys. You can determine which people receive a copy of your e-galley by applying a filter.

I used NetGalley for my third book, *Unexplained Fevers,* as part of a small PR package I bought, so I was able to take advantage of its features at a reduced rate. It is simple to sign up for and use. I believe NetGalley helped me receive a few more reviews online, but I can't say that it would justify a $400 investment. If you are simply looking for a way to distribute your ARCs to the reviewers you are contacting, it's best to do this via email or by using your website. However, your publisher can put up a group of books at a reduced rate. Encourage your publisher to do this!

CHAPTER 23: BOOK BLOG TOURS

Interview With Serena Agusto-Cox

Serena M. Agusto-Cox is a poet whose blog, SavvyVerse & Wit, is a literary review blog and home to the Virtual Poetry Circle. She is also the co-founder of the blog War Through the Generations and owner of Poetic Book Tours. Poetic Book Tours is an online virtual book tour marketing firm for small press authors of fiction, nonfiction, and poetry.

Serena, you've been running your book blog, Savvy Verse & Wit, for some years. Why do you do it? What is the most satisfying part of it?

I've been blogging about books, poetry, and writing since 2007. I started talking about individual poems I read in literary magazines because I felt like others should be reading poetry, too. I think that the genre is often overlooked or even avoided by readers because they have this perception that it is too hard to understand. Then I fell into a book blogging community and received some encouragement from one blogger, Dewey, who has since passed away. She encouraged me to take part in the community and share my thoughts on books, which I did. Since then, I've interacted with men and women throughout the world and shared thoughts on books and poems, and even connected with some who write their own fiction and poetry. That, to me, is the most satisfying part of book blogging—the connections.

You're offering a service now to authors and publishers to help them put together a book blog tour. Can you tell us a little bit about that, and the benefits that a book blog tour can have?

I started Poetic Book Tours at the end of 2014, and my first book blog tours are rolling out this month. When someone wants to create an online book blog tour, we agree on a number of stops for the tour and a mix of reviews, guest posts, and interviews for that tour. Not only do these blog tours give writers more time to work on their writing projects because they are not traveling from bookstore to bookstore and state to state, but they also are able to connect with their readers in an environment that has fewer pressures and constraints on time. Readers and authors can communicate with one another on the blog. It also gives authors a chance to explain their work and inspirations, which many readers are eager to learn about. The costs of an online book tour are far less than traveling on a traditional book tour, and also provide an opportunity to connect with readers on a global scale through the blogs and their social media contacts.

How would you say an online book blog tour compares to a "real life in person" book tour in terms of sales, benefits, etc.?

As I've just started my tour company, I can only tell you what I've learned from my own experience as a book blogger with an affiliate association to Amazon. When readers buy books through the Amazon links on my blog, Savvy Verse & Wit, I can see an immediate sale or even sales a few weeks down the road. These links help me see which books are being purchased because of my reviews, but even those who do not buy through Amazon will often comment that they ordered a book I reviewed through their local bookstore. While online book tours are less costly and time consuming for the author—definite benefits for authors who also have other full-time work—online tours allow them to reach a wider audience, and through tailored packages, they can reach target groups. For instance, poets can reach poetry readers—those who already read poetry—while at the same time, expose new readers to poetry.

As a reviewer yourself, what makes you interested in a certain book, or what raises the chances a book might be featured on your blog?

I have very eclectic tastes, and I love deadlines. I'm probably an anomaly in terms of liking deadlines. I want stories that have not only a unique plot and characters, but also tend to touch me on an emotional or intellectual level. Covers have to be engaging right from the start because honestly, covers that are very blah do not entice me to read the synopsis, which means the synopsis for those books has to be extremely compelling. Usually books that automatically get considered are those written by authors I've read before and loved, poetry, and fiction set during WWI, WWII, and the Vietnam War. I also love books about different countries and cultures, and I'd love to see more about Portugal rather than Spain, for instance. I will read mysteries, but they have to be more than plot driven, unless I'm already invested in the characters from previous books. I am also big on reading translations.

Any advice for poets as they go about trying to get publicity for their new books?

I think poets have a harder time getting coverage, especially in the mainstream media. Beyond that, I think book blogs are a great place to find some decent coverage that will reach an audience interested in new poetry. My first recommendation is to ask poets where they have had coverage for their books in the past, and start with those places. Start looking around the internet for book blogs, and check the archives of their reviews to see if they have ever featured poetry. If that seems like a little too much effort, they could always check out an online book blog tour company, like Poetic Book Tours.

CHAPTER 24: THE SALES SECRET

A "Magic Formula" For Poetry Book Sales

Is there, in fact, a magic formula for selling poetry books? Does it have to do with cults of personality or the quality of the book? How much does the publisher have to do with it? For a book to succeed, sales-wise, you most likely need at least two of the categories I discuss in this chapter.

A Publisher With A PR Presence And Good Distribution

I love indie, one-or-two person publisher teams. They have pluck, they care about the work, and they're lovely to work with, in my experience. But great distribution helps sell books, because if a bookstore can't order your book, it can't sell your book. Some bookstores take consignments, but who has the time to travel the country consigning your own copies of your book? If your publisher can't get your books on Amazon (whatever you think about Amazon), that's going to mean lost sales. If your publisher doesn't have an easy way to purchase books from their website, that's going to mean lost sales. Even in these days of dwindling bookstores, distribution matters. Look for your publisher's distribution channels: Ingram, SPD (Small Press Distribution), Consortium, or a university press. Also, does your publisher have a social media presence? Someone dedicated to PR work? After you get an offer on your book, ask what the publisher can do to help promote it. It benefits both parties to sell the most copies possible.

Charisma

There are three poets I know personally who have sold over 10,000 books. All three of them, though they are fairly diverse individuals, have a couple of things in common. They each radiate good energy, a kind of open charisma that leaves people, if not slightly in love with them, then at least like they've had a nice warm hug. These poets are not necessarily better looking than the rest of us—they just seem to genuinely care about you. If you've never met anyone like that, I'm sorry. Not every poet has this kind of charisma, but I think it's a big plus for book sales.

A Solid Platform

Yes, a platform helps. One of my poet friends sold a lot of books at, of all things, medical conferences, where he gave talks about writing in the context of his medical practice. That's not the kind of opportunity that most authors have, but most of us have specific communities that might be interested in our work. I have a couple of poetry friends who have had good luck selling their books at places like

WonderCon. Platforms can come in a lot of shapes and sizes—your job, your hobbies, and even your alumni associations can be resources for building your audience.

Luck And Buzz

You were probably going to guess this one—*luck* and *buzz*. Someone hears your poem on the radio, and your book is written up in a major newspaper. Someone sees you read at a bookstore and decides to give you a two-book contract at Norton or FSG. Your book wins a major award even though it was a longshot. Somehow, you get the all-important buzz going, and people are reviewing your book, teaching your book, and buying your book. You've won Candyland! I mean, Poetryland! Now go do something nice for other writers to balance your karma.

Some of these positive events we have control over and some we do not. How hard you work to put yourself in the places where you might catch "luck" and "buzz" is up to you because not every effort is going to result in a book contract, prize, or sales. Working with small indie publishers, as I have, means that your book may not have the reach that you hoped for. Working with big publishers can be tough as well (or so I've heard). They don't need poetry to boost their company's sales, and many times, even big publishers expect you to do the majority of promotion. "Luck" and "buzz" do happen from time to time, under the right circumstances, given the right phase of the moon, etc.

CHAPTER 25: FINDING YOUR NUMBERS

Tracking How Many Books You've Sold

Tracking your sales might be one of the most elusive issues in poetry publishing. Don't count on simply getting this information from your publisher—most small press publishers don't issue you the quarterly royalty statements you get from big publishing houses, who have a large, full-time staff and specialized royalty-tracking software. Tracking your book sales is important. Publishers who may consider your future manuscripts might be interested in how many copies your previous book has sold. In this chapter, I'll describe some of the strategies I've used to track my own book sales.

Track Sales Yourself

It seems like obvious advice to tell you to track your own sales. If you are anything like me, you will sell many copies of your book yourself—at readings, festivals, and through your website and social networks. It's important to track these sales. And remember that not all of the books you receive directly from your publisher count as sales. You will probably end up giving many copies away in your marketing efforts, to potential reviewers, or as a thank you to mentors and to blurbers. Giving your book to people is not considered "sales."

A great way to keep track of sales is to use a point-of-sale app on your phone. Such apps as PayPal and Point of Sale by Square, allow you to manually enter and track sales. Square and PayPal also have a credit card reader allowing you to swipe credit cards (for a fee). Here is what my books look like as items in the Point of Sale app:

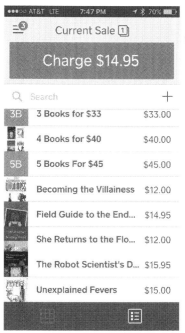

Figure 9: Square point-of-sale app on iPhone

Ask Your Publisher

You can track how many copies of your book you sell yourself, but what about direct sales from the publisher, Amazon, and hopefully bookstores. Your publisher should know your book's numbers. However, this can depend on your book's distribution. Large publishers get BookScan data, which is point-of-sale data collected by the Nielsen company (the same company that does TV ratings). Your small press probably doesn't receive BookScan data, and sometimes smaller publishers aren't as rigorous about tracking sales (especially if you aren't being paid royalties for each book sale). If your publisher pays you royalties, you can usually estimate the number of sales based on your royalty rate. Some publisher pay royalties after expenses, so check your contract.

Look To Amazon

Many poets and publishers aren't fans of Amazon for a variety of reasons, but when it comes to tracking your sales, Amazon may be an author's best friend. Not only do many small press publishers depend on Amazon for print-on-demand services and a large percentage of their sales, but Amazon provides you with a set of author services.

Most importantly, Amazon combines its sales numbers with BookScan numbers and makes them available in their Amazon Author Central portal. Not only can you track your sales in Author Central, Amazon also allows you to create an Amazon Author page using your headshot, bio, a link to your website or blog, and lets you post about your upcoming readings. If your book is available on Amazon (and it really should be), you can just link up to your books, and Amazon does the rest.

To set up your Amazon Author Central account, simply browse to https://authorcentral.amazon.com/ and sign in with your Amazon account. Click on the Books tab, search for your book in Amazon by title or ISBN, then claim it as your book. After you have claimed your book, you can click on the Sales Info tab and select Nielsen BookScan to see your current sales data.

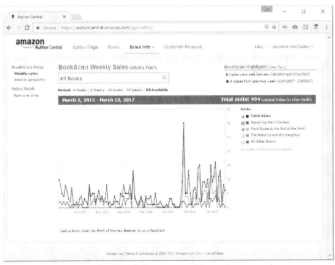

Figure 10: BookScan weekly sales numbers
at Amazon Author Central

Note that you can view sales by time period or geographic location, and if you have multiple books, you see data for specific books.

After setting up your Author Central account, you can also set up an author page by clicking the Author Page menu and adding your bio, blog feed, headshots, events, and videos. All this information is made available to Amazon shoppers when they click your name on Amazon. Below is an example of my Amazon Author page.

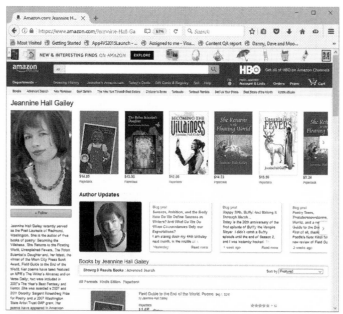

Figure 11: Jeannine Hall Gailey's Amazon Author Page

Why not take advantage of this opportunity to market yourself to Amazon shoppers?

Action Items:

1. Set up a spreadsheet or download a point-of-sale app to track your book sales.

2. Visit the Amazon Author Central site and create your author page. If you have books on Amazon, claim them and review your sales data.

CHAPTER 26: PUBLISHERS SPEAK

Great Advice From Real Publishers

It is useful to hear from the experts—poetry publishers and people who work in sales, marketing, and PR for poetry publishers.

Before I hand over this chapter to the publishers, I'm going to tell you a secret about the poetry publishing world. Depending on your publisher, it might be easy to get information about what they plan to do for your book. Some publishers plan ahead really well (for publicity purposes), and others do not. Some publishers keep better track of individual book sales than others. (One friend of mine publishes with a respected small press whose editor confesses to not keeping track at all.) There are also stories of publishers who never give timely reports on sales or royalties to their authors, in spite of the contractual agreement. I have had mostly good experiences with royalties with all of my presses—one press gave me an advance, unheard of in the poetry world—and my publishers have all been responsive to queries. But this experience may vary, and I want to warn you about this up front. Many poets have been disappointed by non-responsive publishers, and even poets with sterling publishers complain about the lack of support they get—just go to any cocktail party at AWP, if you

174

don't believe me. You can't expect publishers to do everything perfectly. Publishing poetry books is often a labor of love and not a profitable enterprise. If you want to be a beloved author of a certain press, do everything you can for your book.

The following interviews contain very valuable information—inside information, you might say, from the heart of the poetry publishing beast itself.

Interview With Kelly Forsythe

Kelly Forsythe, previously the Director of Publicity at Copper Canyon Books, was kind enough to answer a few questions—and give a few tips—from this successful and prestigious poetry press.

What is the number one thing you wish your authors knew about promoting their poetry books before they signed up to publish with you?

I wish that our authors had greater accessibility / an easier way to discover and set up readings, lectures, class visits, etc. I think *Poets & Writers* just put out a great resource for this, actually—so I wish that in advance of acceptance or publication, this kind of information was more widely known and used.

I've discussed in this book about how selling 1,000 copies is pretty good for a poetry book and how 10,000 is a "magical" number of sales. Some of your titles have gone far past the 10,000 mark! What do you think makes the difference between "pretty" successful poetry books and "magically" successful poetry books? (Aside from winning the Pulitzer Prize and being the US Poet Laureate, which I'm sure do not hurt!)

I do think strong reviews or interviews in major publications help. For example, media venues such as *The New York Times Book Review* are powerful sources because they increase the visibility of the title, and therefore people remember it longer, remember the author's name, purchase it immediately or purchase it later because the review spoke to them—so that is one thing. I also think strong academic marketing is important . . . building relationships and communicating consistently with professors and teachers, which is something anyone can do, not just publicists. I think spreading out the social media coverage of a book, i.e. scheduling spaces between posts about reviews or interviews of a particular title, helps. It encourages a **continued** interest in the book beyond just the two or three months after it's released.

What have you learned working in public relations for Copper Canyon Press that you think has affected the way the way you think about writing and publishing poetry?

Almost everything I thought about publishing poetry

has changed since I began working with Copper Canyon. I've learned that community is exceptionally meaningful—an author's personal community, a press's community of readers . . . the *community* is vital to not only the success of a collection but also the success of a given publisher. I've also learned that energy is contagious, and if you're authentically excited about a book of poems (whether your own or if you're working in publicity and pitching a title), that excitement usually translates to your peers, contacts, friends, family. I also think I've learned that the most effective professional relationships are the ones where underneath you genuinely build a connection, appreciation, respect and admiration for one another. In other words: friendship.

Interview With Marie Gauthier

Marie Gauthier is the author of *Hunger All Inside* and the Director of Sales and Marketing for Tupelo Press. She also runs The Collected Poets reading series. Marie shares some of her expertise about the ways you can help your press sell your book of poetry, how to connect with readers, and how the book industry is changing.

As the Director of Sales and Marketing for Tupelo Press, what kind of PR would you say works the best for poetry book sales? Review copies, PR kits, postcards, emails? I know Tupelo has also created "Study Guides" for its books, among other innovative ideas.

The idea is to make it as easy as possible for people to support you and buy your book. For a straight-up sales bump, nothing beats a mention on the internet —via social media, or a well-designed email— something easily shared, with a cover image and link to purchase.

At Tupelo, we've redoubled our efforts to work with our authors on the Reader's Companions (RCs). Available as free PDFs on the Tupelo website, they're written by the authors themselves, and then edited with just as much care as the books we publish. The RCs are very useful for attracting course adoptions, or poet-in-the-school programs, as well as the general reader who's simply interested in a deeper engagement.

Review copies are still really important. Reviews can be long in coming, but attention builds on itself, one review leads to another as more readers find your work. While we're judicious and realistic, we still send as many review copies as we can.

You have to take the long view. Poetry sales and prose sales are different animals. A poetry book doesn't "age" on the bookstore (virtual or actual) shelf at the same accelerated pace as a prose book.

What's the one thing that you think authors can do to help their publishers boost their books sales? And what's the one thing they should avoid?

Maintain a website. Link to your publisher. Simple things that make it easy for potential readers to find and buy your book. Also, when you think about giving readings, consider asking friends or family to host a salon, or book party. Sometimes people can be intimidated by the idea of a poetry reading, but will attend something less formal and more their idea of fun. Less book, more party. Make a mini-book tour of it if you can, traveling from home to home, party to party.

Avoid spending all your review copy capital by giving away free copies to family and friends! Give them a cut rate if you like, but allow them to acknowledge the hard work you've put into your art by paying you, or your publisher, for it.

How different was it for you to do PR for your own book compared to doing PR for the books at Tupelo Press?

Oh, it's so much more difficult to promote your own work than it is to promote someone else's. All the angst and insecurity is your own. Doing PR requires a sense of proportion and a sense of humor. For yourself, exponentially so.

As PR and publishing businesses are changing (social media, distribution changes, Amazon, etc.) how are you changing what you do for poetry books in particular?

Tupelo is different from most small presses in that we have commission sales reps who make sales calls on independent bookstores all across the country. In addition to distributing our books via SPD, Ingram, and Baker & Taylor, we actively self-distribute, and manage our relationship with Amazon directly. We've taken a very hands-on approach to handling sales, and while it's been a positive experience, it continues to be a challenge.

Okay, here's the real question. Can you discuss how hard you think it is to sell a book of poetry, and what poets and publishers can do to make it a little easier?

It is hard to sell a book of poetry. At full price. To strangers. And relations! You can't take poor sales to heart. But all things being equal (quality of the work, etc.), I've noted that the poets whose books sell regularly tend to be active members of some sort of poetry community. Translation: poets who take joy in all aspects of poetry, who are interested in other poets and other poems beyond their own, who seek out ways to be involved. As in most things in life, you should be giving as much, if not more, than you receive. Which is to say, sales are a natural progression of your own engagement with others. For example, someone who spends a portion of her time writing reviews of poetry books is more likely to find her own book reviewed. It's not about networking, but about having a personal stake in the poetry community.

More Tips!

I also talked to the publisher of my first book, Tom C. Hunley of Steel Toe Books, to see if he had tips for poetry authors. Here are some of his suggestions:

- People are more likely to buy your book if you have the presence to bring the poems alive for them. People do sometimes judge books by their covers, so good cover design is important, but they're more likely to buy a book from you at a reading than from a bookstore.

- As a publisher, I've found that "project" books (or books with easily-summarized, cohesive descriptions—books that are about something) are easier to sell than loosely-collected poems featuring a poet's best poems written in a given period of time. The latter type of book often has better individual poems and is for me, personally, often a more rewarding read, but at bookfairs, it's an easier sell if I can make a short, clear pitch, e.g. "This poet uses female superheroes and mythological figures as a vehicle for representing female empowerment" or "These poems are about pregnancy, childrearing, and post-partum depression."

Action Items:

1. Have a conversation with your publisher about what they expect from you in terms of promoting your book, what they expect to do for your book, and what you can both afford. Being up front with your options allows you and your publisher to remain realistic in terms of expectations. A clear understanding also motivates you and your publisher to step in when the other cannot.

2. If your publisher has someone in charge of PR, please take advantage of this. If you have requests, be sure these requests are reasonable—don't ask for 100 things at once or expect the PR person to book you on TV morning shows). Offer to participate as much as you can in the promotion of your book.

CHAPTER 27: INVESTING IN YOURSELF

When To Help Your Publisher By Spending Your Own Money

Many authors are surprised to find out they might be expected to shell out some of their own cash to help promote their first book. When I started out as an author, I bartered web skills for author copies and wheedled wonderful cover art out of talented friends for only nominal fees. My first book's publisher and I split the costs of ads in places like *Poets & Writers*. Some publishers require that the author pre-sell or purchase a certain number of copies. (I'm not a huge fan of that.) Plan on setting aside a certain amount of money to buy author copies, pay for a few out-of-town readings, and help out with ads and swag.

Author Copies

Most poets only get a few author copies in their contract, usually between 10 and 20 books, unless they've received an award that includes copies or negotiated more books up front. Because of friends, family, mentors, and blurbers, you will find that those 10-20 copies do not go very far.

Many authors will work with their publishers to buy extra author copies up front, which they plan to sell at readings, send to reviewers, or give to family members as gifts. It is a common practice to send author copies to everyone who helped you in writing the book, gave you a blurb, created your cover art, etc. You may want extra copies for family members. Try not to give away too many books to extended family and friends; it's a temptation, especially with your first book. Most publishers will allow you to buy a certain number of copies for a discount, and sometimes the discount increases with the number of copies you buy.

Ads: Online And In Print

I've shared the cost with other authors and publishers to buy ads in *Poets & Writers* and on *Verse Daily*, and I've purchased ads that target specific communities, like the Horror Writers Association newsletter. I've never been sure exactly what kind of return on investment buying ads for poetry books has (it's hard to measure), but I do think that opportunities for readers, reviewers, professors, and editors to see a mention of your book could ignite their interest.

Swag And Postcards With Postage

Sometimes your publisher will cover the cost of postcards, or at least the postage to send out your book postcards. Remember when I talked about bookmarks, magnets, and other kinds of swag? Those costs will probably be on you.

Book Tour Costs

Most poetry publishers won't be able to afford to send you on a countrywide tour, I'm sorry to say. Occasionally they will be able to help out, either with costs or doing something extra, like putting you up in their own home, but most poets travel on their own dime.

It's important to consider costs when you think about where you want to do readings. If you're on a limited budget, or have limited time, you might want to keep your readings within a short driving distance from home. I always recommend a reading in your hometown. Stay with friends and relatives and encourage them to attend your reading. Plan some kind of get-together afterwards. If you are invited to a conference, festival, or university for a reading, be sure to ask if there's an honorarium and if travel costs will be covered. Some poets organize readings for trips they have already planned (such as a trip home to visit family or a trip to a city with a great bookstore). It's sort of the "feeding two birds with one scone" idea.

CHAPTER 28: EYE ON THE PRIZE

Entering Published Book Prizes

Many times new authors try to win a "first book" prize. These prizes award you publication, some prize money, and maybe a reading. There is also a class of prizes offered for already-published manuscripts—the Pulitzer Prize and Nobel Prize fall into this category, but there are smaller prizes that are included in this category as well. You will want to work with your publisher to make sure your book gets submitted to the appropriate published book prizes. Winning or being a finalist in these prizes can do everything from providing a little bump in sales to increasing your visibility to helping you become a more "established" writer.

Talk to your publisher about their budget for entrance fees and how many copies they are willing to put towards prizes. Some publishers have generous policies, others not so much. If your publisher is only willing to enter your book into a certain number of contests, make a list of the contests (that don't require a fee) that you think you have the best chance to win. You can offer to pay some of the fees yourself. Some contests do not allow authors to send in their own work, so you will need your publisher's support for certain prizes.

Some good prizes to consider for your published poetry book might include: The Foreword Indies, the Julie Suk Award, the National Book Critics Circle Award, the Erik Hoffer Prize, National Book Award, and the Pulitzer Prize. Also check into your state's book awards—some states offer prizes for writers who have lived in that state for a certain number of years. You might also want to search for prizes that suit you and your book. There are specific prizes for different groups—the Lambda Literary Award for LGBTQ poets or awards for speculative work, like the Elgin Award from the Science Fiction Poetry Association and the Horror Writers Award in Poetry.

Action Item:

Research book contests for already-published books. There are contests for poets of a certain age, poets with first or second book, or for mid-career poets. Basically, there's a wide array of prizes, and you should narrow them down to those which are the best fit for you and your book. I have included contest information in the resources list at the end of this book.

CHAPTER 29: PACE YOURSELF

Poetry Book Promotion Is A Marathon, Not A Sprint

As I'm writing this, I'm in month six of the debut of my fourth book. Month six is tough. Most of the early reviews are already out, but the late reviews aren't out yet. There will probably be a lull in readings and sales. By now, I feel like I've have posted about my book way too many times on social media.

By the time your book has been out for several months, it's good to work on your long-term strategy. The number of positive reviews on places like Amazon and Goodreads are important. Ask your friends or colleagues to review your book on Amazon and Goodreads if they've sent you well wishes or told you how much they like the book. Remind them that the review doesn't need to be long or complicated, just a quick sentence on why they love your work. Receiving a good number of positive reviews will help you reach other readers. Asking for reviews can feel humiliating, but swallow your pride and do it. Also, Amazon rewards books that have more reviews—you are more likely to be recommended when someone buys a book similar to yours.

So Much For The Afterglow

After the publication of your book, be prepared for a little letdown. What, your world didn't change the minute your book came out? That's totally normal. Maybe consider having a new project in the works before your book comes out, so you have something to distract yourself from checking your Amazon rank fifty times a day.

There are a couple of odd phenomena that sometimes occur right after your book is finally published. One of them is letdown; the other is a sense of exhaustion, hatred of your book, and complete resistance to doing anything to promote your book.

Letdown is natural. You've spent years of your life writing and revising your book, sending it out to publishers, editing it with the publisher, doing some prep work to set up your readings and promotions before publication, and now—whew! It's over. The books have been delivered in their cardboard box to your doorstep. You're finished! Right? No…

The effort of having to pick yourself up after the publication of your book is often a surprise to new authors, and even to repeat authors. You have to psych yourself up because now is your (and your book's) time to shine! If you suddenly feel disbelief in yourself, your work, and your book, please call a supportive friend and get yourself a pep talk. Have a party and invite only people who love you. Do what you need to do to overcome that initial letdown if it happens to you. It's a great accomplishment, publishing a book of poetry, one that many poets never have the opportunity to celebrate.

You might also experience a weird feeling of resistance when it comes to promoting your book. Overcoming this mental block is crucial. You've put immense effort into this book! Don't let it be ignored. You want your poetry in the hands of readers, reviewers, press people, reporters, and the general public. And that doesn't happen without some effort on the part of the poet.

Get Out Of Town

By the end of your first year of promoting your book, you will likely have exhausted all of the opportunities for giving local readings, and most of your family, friends, and writing community will have your book. You need to look for new opportunities—perhaps out of town.

Is there a festival or conference you would really like to attend? A city you haven't visited yet on your book tour? Look through the section on conferences in *Poet's Market* or the writers' conferences and festivals issue of *Poets & Writers* to get some ideas. There are some conferences you can apply for directly by sending in a form and a copy of your book or by querying. Participation in other conferences is by invitation only. The better and more prestigious the conference or festival, the more renowned you will need to be to get an invite.

If there is a local or regional writers/poetry conference in your area, offer to teach a class or give a reading there. By being a reader or presenter, you will usually have your book sold alongside the other participants. However, if you show up as only an attendee trying to interest other attendees in your book, you may be disappointed.

When applying to festivals and conferences, remember to always include your headshot. It's also a good idea to have sample audio, and ideally video, of you reading your work.

Action Items:

1. In terms of the longevity and staying power of your book, make a list of promotional and marketing actions that you can do three months, six months, nine months, and a year after your book comes out.

2. How do you keep up the momentum of

promoting your book without becoming exhausted? Everyone has to find their own energy level and ability to reach out. Plan some down time, and then get out there and do some promotion each quarter, or, if you like, at the beginning of each season.

CHAPTER 30: WIN IN THE CLASSROOM

How To Get Your Book Taught

One way to achieve higher sales for your poetry book is to have it adopted as part of a class, especially at the college level. But how do you do that?

As Marie Gauthier mentioned in her interview, sometimes publishers will put together a "study guide" to go with your book in order to market it specifically to teachers and professors. If your publisher isn't doing this, you can do it yourself. You can offer in-person visits to local universities, colleges, and schools, or Skype visits. Many authors lecture at local community colleges, give workshops and readings at universities across the country by using Skype, FaceTime, and Google Hangouts. It's fun and rewarding working with students and instructors.

Heidi Czerwiec, Associate Professor at the University of North Dakota, says:

I've ordered books for my class to discuss because poets have offered on Facebook to Skype into classrooms if you teach their book—if it's a book/poet I already love, I'm sold.

Sometimes your book is chosen to be taught because of reviews and ads, good word-of-mouth, and a catchy title or cover seen at a bookfair. Maybe instructors are looking for a book of villanelles, or a book on horror tropes in movies, or a book that includes WWII history. Sometimes you get lucky.

Having a network of friends that includes people who teach is a plus. When possible, I send out "desk copies" to instructors who've taught my books in the past or who seem interested in teaching my books in the future. But remember how many author copies we usually receive from our press—10-20 books. If you have an e-galley, send it to some friends who teach. Sending it before the book's release is a smart idea as well. The e-galley also works great when you are out of review copies and ARCs. When sending your books to an instructor, suggest what kind of classes the book would be useful for. For example, mention how your book focuses on ecological poems if you are sending it to an environmental-focused instructor. If your book has a feminist message, maybe send it to Women Studies teachers. Make sure to target your cover letter to the specific instructor. And remember to offer a visit by Skype or in person if you can. This has the potential to give you a steady source of book sales.

CHAPTER 31: GO CLUBBING

Capture The Sales Power Of Book Clubs

Another more intimate way to sell books—and to meet new audiences—is by offering to visit book clubs. Book clubs do not read poetry as often as they do fiction, as a rule, but they may take a look at a poetry collection with a relevant theme—a mystery book club may look at a poetry book with a film noir theme, for instance, or a women's book club may choose a poetry book about the experience of motherhood.

Visiting book clubs may not seem as "big picture" as visiting a college class or doing a large bookstore reading, but I have found that the quality of discussion and audience engagement with the book are much higher than at your average reading.

A poet friend of mine, Susan Rich, author of *Cures Include Travel* and *The Alchemist's Kitchen*, designed "A Poet at Your Table" as a way to introduce poets to area book clubs, and it has been a success. A group of Seattle area poets have signed up to be part of "A Poet at Your Table." Local book clubs can look through the poets' pages provided on the website for "A Poet at Your Table" and read about their books to determine which poet might be a good fit for their book club. You can set up something similar in your area. Here's Susan's description of the project:

I started the group "A Poet At Your Table" after eavesdropping on a conversation. I was at the Miami Book Festival, listening in as two novelists started talking about their experiences visiting book groups. Perhaps they exaggerated, as fiction writers sometimes do, but the people they met, the dinners they were invited to, and the magic of conversations centered around one's own writing seemed a kind of literary heaven. "A Poet At Your Table" is essentially a clearinghouse for poets and for book clubs. I wanted to promote the simple concept that poets will also visit book clubs.

In my experience, book groups can be a bit cautious of having the poet at the table when poetry might be new to the group (most book groups seem to stick with fiction or nonfiction). However, after contacting libraries, area bookstores, and putting the word out to friends who have book groups, the idea is working! Local groups who have brought a poet to their table often come back for another poet the next year. Our web page (poet.susanrich.net/for-book-groups/) lets people see which poets are available. We have also had requests from colleges and writing groups. This is our group's 6th year. Every community is different so feel free to adapt this idea for your own community.

CHAPTER 32: PR CALENDAR

One Year Before Launch:

☐ Begin by building an online presence: create a basic website and get a professional head shot photo taken.

☐ Start a blog now so that you can begin building an audience for your work. Mention your upcoming book periodically.

☐ Start building a social media following by creating Twitter and Facebook accounts if you don't already have them.

☐ Visit local art galleries to see local artwork and meet artists.

Six Months Before Launch:

☐ Start contacting bookstores or other venues to schedule your book launch reading, party, and other book events. This is not too early! Many bookstores and universities book out six months or more in advance.

☐ If you've got e-galleys from your publisher, this is the time to start sending them to professional review venues.

☐ Continue building a social media following, and be sure to post material related to your book—deciding on cover art, author photos, a new blurb! This lets your audience share your excitement for the book.

☐ Some publishers want you to get your own blurbs and cover art while some want to be in control of both. Be sure that you have an established timeline with your publisher if it's up to you to get blurbs and art. In consultation with your press, send out e-galleys to potential blurbers—former professors, mentors, writers you admire and feel you share an aesthetic with.

Three Months Before Launch:

☐ Start planning your book launch reading(s) and party (parties) now. Hopefully you have already booked a place for the reading and the party afterwards, which sometimes requires a deposit to reserve a restaurant or bar.

☐ At this point, you should work with your publisher to create and finish a sell sheet and PR kit.

☐ Start contacting potential reviewers and review outlets with your e-galley, sell sheet, and PR kit.

☐ Start planning your book tour, even if you're not totally sure how many places you want/can afford to visit. Start small—a nearby community—and call your favorite bookstore to find out if you can book a reading.

☐ Design and order your book postcards with your cover art and basic info about your book—ISBN, price, publisher, where to order.

One Month Before Launch:

☐ Send out postcards to your mailing list. Include the book's launch date and if possible, a personal greeting and note on each postcard. (*Hi Grandma! Super excited about my book coming out! Hope you can make it to the reading!*)

☐ For your first reading, inquire with the bookstore or venue if they have ordered your book from a distributor or if they would prefer you to bring copies to sell on consignment. Ask if you can do anything to help promote the reading, like sending out links to the event and placing posters around the community.

☐ Design an email announcement to send out to your email list about one week before your book comes out.

☐ Order your book "swag"—this can be bookmarks, magnets, etc. I ordered toy robot rings to put on cupcakes at the launch of *The Robot Scientist's*

Daughter, and my friend, Natasha Kochicheril Moni, ordered anatomically-correct chocolate hearts for her book, *The Cardiologist's Daughter*. Find something to make the event memorable!

Book Launch!

☐ This is where all your hard work pays off. Do your launch reading(s) and celebrate, possibly multiple times, with friends and family. Drink some champagne or sparkling cider, and give out your swag! Also, bring extra copies of your book, just in case there is a problem with the bookstore ordering its copies. I recommend always keeping at least 20-30 books in your car or in your personal inventory for those "just in case" moments.

☐ Celebrate! Hug your book. Take copious photos of it and post them—you hugging it, famous poets holding it. This is like the obnoxious baby photos everyone posts, but for your new book! Okay, maybe only do this in moderation.

Three Months After Launch:

☐ At this point you should still be writing to potential review outlets and scheduling book tour readings. Your book promotion process will probably last a full year, if not longer. And if it has success, you'll find yourself more in demand and busier six months after the book comes out than six months before!

Six Months After Launch:

☐ Talk to your publisher about what book prizes they plan to submit your book to. Ask if you can help (if you have the time and money) and submit to as many reputable prizes as you can. Pulitzer, sure, but these are some freakishly low odds. It's better to submit to your state or city's book prize, for instance.

One Year On:

☐ Don't get discouraged if you haven't met all your goals for your book promotion in the first year. Keep scheduling readings and promoting your book on social media. Remember that your yearling book still has some legs. With the speed of journals publishing reviews, it can take up to two years to launch a book of poetry. As reviews roll in, make sure you're keeping track of them. Send links to your publisher as they may use the reviews to promote your book. Each review is a chance to renew people's interest on social media.

CHAPTER 33: GO AND DO SOME PR

How To Get Your Small Press Book Some, Well, Press

I've talked about some statistics indicating that most small press poetry books sell less than 1,000 copies—sometimes less than 300 copies. You love your book and you hope other people get the chance to read it. So how do small press authors help make that happen?

You already know that a book's work is not finished the minute it's written, the moment it's sold, or the moment it appears in bookstores or on Amazon. You already know you can't simply say: "I wrote this book, and it's the publisher's job to sell it."

Here are some reminders of where to spend your time and energy going forward with your book.

Go Social

Use Facebook and Twitter as much as possible. I have found Twitter, in particular, a wonderful way to connect with new readers—it only takes time, not money. Create thoughtful Facebook posts that offer something of you and your personality to your readers with a little bit of promotion in between. Go on guest blogs and do interviews. Branch out as new social media tools become available.

Ask For Help

Befriend book bloggers and ask for some aid. I have friends who blog about books because I tend to like those kinds of people, but I'm usually reticent to ask them to do anything for my book. Do you feel the same way? Is that good/modesty, or bad/getting-in-your-own-way? Do you ask your friends and family to help get the word out about your book? Sometimes I do, and sometimes I don't. It's always good to ask.

Do Readings

Do at least a few readings. If you can get a reading on the radio, do it. Readings make poems come alive for people, and they help you connect to an audience—it's a small audience that might care about poetry, true, but it's out there.

Mail Your Postcards

Remember to send out your book postcards to the mailing list you put together of people who are interested in your work. And you have put together your mailing list, right? This is, again, one of the most successful ways to sell books to people you already know. Aunt Thelma loves getting postcards, and you already know she wants a copy of your book!

Get Your Book Reviewed

As a reviewer, I've said before that I'm not sure it drives sales, but it's important to send out review copies, as many as possible, to the big reviewers and the small reviewers. Word of mouth does drive sales, and if one extra person looks at your book because of a review, it'll be worth it. And it might make an impact when it comes to post-publication book prizes.

Enter Contests For Published Books

Ask your publisher to send your book to as many of these contests and prizes as they can afford. If they are unable to do this, then send your book to some contests on your own dime.

Good Luck!

Thank you for reading this book. I hope you have found some useful tips about marketing and promotion. Be sure to reread *PR for Poets* when your next book comes out! Good luck!

ADDITIONAL RESOURCES: ONLINE AND IN PRINT

Platform

- Robert Lee Brewer's Guide to How to Build or Maintain Your Writer Platform: http://www.writersdigest.com/editor-blogs/there-are-no-rules/improve-your-writing-platform-author-platform
- The Brand Called You by Tom Peters: www.fastcompany.com/28905/brand-called-you
- 7 Ways Authors Waste Time "Building Platform" on Social Media: annerallen.com/7-ways-authors-waste-time-building/
- WorldCat.org

Publishers And Contests

- *Poet's Market 2018* (or any edition from the last few years): These books, besides being repositories of literary magazines and publishers, contain numerous articles on such topics as getting reviews to building community to building platforms to social media. It's well worth the twenty bucks or so.
- Rachel Dacus's list of poetry manuscript publishers: www.dacushome.com/Poetry%20Book%20Publishers.htm

- Tom Holmes's list of poetry manuscript publishers: thelinebreak.wordpress.com/2012/06/16/presses-with-open-readings-for-full-length-poetry-manuscripts/#comment-1345

Other Useful Resources And Websites
- NewPages.com
- Net Galley: netgalley.com
- Amazon Author Central: authorcentral.amazon.com
- Book Reviewing Newspaper Info: http://bookmarketingbestsellers.com/newspaper-book-review-editors

Buying Ads
- *Poets and Writers*: www.pw.org/about-us/advertise
- Verse Daily: www.versedaily.org/support.shtml
- Poetry Daily: poems.com/support_sponsor.php

Social Media Information
- Book Reviewers On Instagram: www.forbes.com/sites/jopiazza/2017/05/25/instagram-bookstagrammers-selling-books/#282b324c727b

Prizes For Published Books
- Contests for already-published books on Bernadette Geyer's website: https://bernadettegeyer.com/2017/05/07/contests-for-already-published-poetry-books-updated

Book Clubs
- Information about poetry book groups by Susan Rich: poet.susanrich.net/for-book-groups/

Swag And Printers
- VistaPrint: vistaprint.com
- MOO Cards: moo.com
- CafePress: cafepress.com

Interviews With Poets And Writing Tips
- Robert Lee Brewer's Poetic Asides Blog: writersdigest.com/editor-blogs/poetic-asides
- There Are No Rules Blog from Writer's Digest: www.writersdigest.com/editor-blogs/there-are-no-rules

Jeannine Hall Gailey served as the second Poet Laureate of Redmond, Washington. She is the author of five books of poetry: *Becoming the Villainess, She Returns to the Floating World, Unexplained Fevers, The Robot Scientist's Daughter,* and *Field Guide to the End of the World,* winner of the Moon City Press Book Prize and the SFPA's Elgin Award. Her work has been featured on NPR's The Writer's Almanac, Verse Daily, and in *The Year's Best Fantasy and Horror.* Her poems have appeared in *American Poetry Review, Notre Dame Review,* and *Prairie Schooner.* She has a B.S. in Biology and an M.A. in English from the University of Cincinnati and her MFA in Poetry from Pacific University. She spent four years teaching in the MFA program for National University, worked fifteen years as a corporate writing manager, and worked in publishing as an Acquisition Editor for Microsoft Press. Her website is www.webbish6.com. Twitter handle: @webbish6.

Publications by Two Sylvias Press:

The Daily Poet:
Day-By-Day Prompts For Your Writing Practice
by Kelli Russell Agodon and Martha Silano (Print and eBook)

The Daily Poet Companion Journal (Print)

Fire On Her Tongue:
An Anthology of Contemporary Women's Poetry
edited by Kelli Russell Agodon and Annette Spaulding-Convy
(Print and eBook)

The Poet Tarot and Guidebook:
A Deck Of Creative Exploration (Print)

PR For Poets: A Guidebook to Publicity and Marketing
by Jeannine Hall Gailey (Print and eBook)

Appalachians Run Amok
Winner of the 2016 Two Sylvias Press Wilder Prize
by Adrian Blevins (Print and eBook)

Killing Marias
by Claudia Castro Luna (Print and eBook)

The Ego and the Empiricist
Finalist for the 2016 Two Sylvias Press Chapbook Prize
by Derek Mong (Print and eBook)

The Authenticity Experiment
by Kate Carroll de Gutes (Print and eBook)

Mytheria, Finalist 2015 Two Sylvias Press Wilder Prize
by Molly Tenenbaum (Print and eBook)

Arab in Newsland
Winner of the 2016 Two Sylvias Press Chapbook Prize
by Lena Khalaf Tuffaha (Print and eBook)

The Blue Black Wet of Wood
Winner of the 2015 Two Sylvias Press Wilder Prize
by Carmen R. Gillespie (Print and eBook)

Fire Girl: Essays on India, America, and the In-Between
by Sayantani Dasgupta (Print and eBook)

Blood Song
by Michael Schmeltzer (Print and eBook)

Naming The No-Name Woman,
Winner of the 2015 Two Sylvias Press Chapbook Prize
by Jasmine An (Print and eBook)

Community Chest
by Natalie Serber (Print)

Phantom Son: A Mother's Story of Surrender
by Sharon Estill Taylor (Print and eBook)

What The Truth Tastes Like
by Martha Silano (Print and eBook)

landscape/heartbreak
by Michelle Peñaloza (Print and eBook)

Earth, Winner of the 2014 Two Sylvias Press Chapbook Prize
by Cecilia Woloch (Print and eBook)

The Cardiologist's Daughter
by Natasha Kochicheril Moni (Print and eBook)

She Returns to the Floating World
by Jeannine Hall Gailey (Print and eBook)

Hourglass Museum
by Kelli Russell Agodon (eBook)

Cloud Pharmacy
by Susan Rich (eBook)

Dear Alzheimer's: A Caregiver's Diary & Poems
by Esther Altshul Helfgott (eBook)

Listening to Mozart: Poems of Alzheimer's
by Esther Altshul Helfgott (eBook)

Crab Creek Review 30th Anniversary Issue
featuring Northwest Poets (eBook)
edited by Kelli Russell Agodon and Annette Spaulding-Convy

Please visit Two Sylvias Press (www.twosylviaspress.com) for information on purchasing our print books, eBooks, writing tools, and for submission guidelines for our annual book prizes. Created with the belief that great writing is good for the world.

Made in the USA
Coppell, TX
30 March 2021

52714081R10134